FREEDOM UNLEASHED

Freedom Unleashed

Challenging the World's Views and Breaking Barriers

by
Dennis Brown

PITTSBURGH, PENNSYLVANIA 15238

The contents of this work, including, but not limited to, the accuracy of events, people, and places depicted; opinions expressed; permission to use previously published materials included; and any advice given or actions advocated are solely the responsibility of the author, who assumes all liability for said work and indemnifies the publisher against any claims stemming from publication of the work.

All Rights Reserved
Copyright © 2024 by Dennis Brown

No part of this book may be reproduced or transmitted, downloaded, distributed, reverse engineered, or stored in or introduced into any information storage and retrieval system, in any form or by any means, including photocopying and recording, whether electronic or mechanical, now known or hereinafter invented without permission in writing from the publisher.

RoseDog Books
585 Alpha Drive, Suite 103
Pittsburgh, PA 15238
Visit our website at www.rosedogbookstore.com

ISBN: 979-8-89127-647-5
eISBN: 979-8-89127-145-6

Contents

The Introduction vii
    Freedom Unleashed: Challenging the World's Views
    and Breaking Barriers

Chapter 1 1
    Identifying and Defining Harmful Worldviews

Chapter 2 5
    Worldview of a Fixed Mindset and its Limitations

Chapter 3 11
    Worldviews that Drive Fear-Driven Mentality

Chapter 4 19
    The Hollow Pursuit of Materialism and Consumerism

Chapter 5 29
    The Downward Spiral of Pessimism and Negativity

Chapter 6 37
    The Barrier of Ethnocentrism and Prejudice

Chapter 7 47
    The Power of Reflection: A Mirror to the Self

Chapter 8 57
    The LIGHT Pathway (Luminary Foundation, Inclusive
    Bonds, Generous Empathy, Harmonious Evolution,
    and Transformative Growth)

Chapter 9 71
    Inclusive Bonds: The Web (Building and Maintaining
    Relationships)

Chapter 10 97
    Generous Empathy - The Oasis (Developing Compassion
    and Understanding)

Chapter 11 109
    Harmonious Evolution - The Transition (Envisioning and
    implementing change)

Chapter 12 125
    Transformative Growth - The Peak (Embracing
    personal growth and Development)
Chapter 13 151
    Legacy Unveiled: Leaving a Lasting Mark
Chapter 14 163
    The Dark Side of Power and Money: Confronting
    Divisions and Corruption
Chapter 15 177
    Breaking the Chains: A Call to Action
Conclusion 191

The Introduction

Freedom Unleashed: Challenging the World's Views and Breaking Barriers

Have you ever found yourself yearning for more in the bustling chaos of our lives? A deep, unshakeable sense of dissatisfaction settling into the core of your being, coloring every aspect of your existence—career, family, friends, even your spiritual journey? If so, you are not alone. I, too, have wrestled with this relentless hunger for fulfillment and embarked on a transformative odyssey.

During this journey, I learned about the lives of people from many different cultures and backgrounds. I did this to figure out the invisible strands that connect us all, but often leave us empty. What I discovered was astonishing: our worldviews, shaped by the stories we were told and the experiences we lived through, profoundly impact our potential for growth in these essential dimensions of life. Our upbringing can inadvertently confine us, leaving our lives unbalanced and fraught with challenges. Our goal should be to unearth the hidden barriers that hold us back and learn how to break free from these shackles, ultimately achieving a harmonious balance in our careers, families, friends, and spiritual pursuits.

Growing up in Omaha, Nebraska, during the dynamic 1970s and through the onset of the new millennium, the love of my middle-class family nurtured me. My mother, a homemaker, and my father, a blue-collar worker, wove a tapestry of values, beliefs, and aspirations that formed the backdrop of my life. However, the generational transmission of worldviews can create invisible chains that impact our decisions and identities, only sometimes to our benefit. Imagine a world where we could break free from these invisible chains and live a whole life, spiritually and professionally, with our families and friends.

Like most parents, my parents told my siblings and me to dream big. They told me I could be anything I wanted, like a doctor, lawyer, engineer, athlete, or actor, all high-profile jobs. Our hearts were full of ambition and potential, but there was also unspoken pressure to fit society's narrow idea of success. What if we could define success in our way, free from others' expectations? Through the turbulence of adolescence, I embarked on an odyssey of self-discovery, questioning the values and beliefs instilled in me. This journey exposed me to diverse cultures and viewpoints, leading me to embrace a new vision of success rooted in biblical leadership principles.

Imagine a life where interdependence among spirituality, family, friends, and career determines success. By caring for these relationships, we can achieve a profound sense of accomplishment beyond societal expectations. Honoring our values and beliefs enables us to rise above societal pressure and live a fulfilling, happy life. This transformational journey has shaped my identity and world perspective, leading me to implement a step-by-step process to cultivate inner resilience, allowing us to navigate life's challenges gracefully.

Bringing together spirituality, family, friends, and work can make our lives full of meaning, connection, and fulfillment. This holistic approach to success challenges the traditional, often materialistic, definition and encourages individuals to look beyond external markers of achievement. It empowers people to define success on their terms, fosters an environment where unique passions and dreams can be pursued, and maintains balance and well-being in all areas of life.

Imagine embracing this revolutionary approach to success, boldly forging your destiny by nourishing your spiritual life, deepening connections with loved ones and friends, and pursuing a meaningful career. This investment brings satisfaction beyond material possessions or external validation. Consider the impact on future generations as we teach children to value authenticity, empathy, patience, and balance rather than chasing society's ever-shifting standards of success. Together, we can challenge the status quo, shatter convention's shackles, and create a world where everyone has the freedom to explore their unique path to happiness and fulfillment.

Chapter 1

Identifying and Defining Harmful Worldviews

Numerous invisible worldview chains that affect our thoughts and, among other things, our ability to achieve a fulfilled life in terms of our careers, relationships with family and friends, and spirituality can bind us. Indeed, people can be under the influence of several worldviews simultaneously, which happens every day. These worldviews can often intertwine and interact in complex ways, shaping our thoughts, feelings, and behaviors in many dimensions. This diversity adds another layer of complexity to our endeavor to understand and transform our worldviews.

Just as a house can be built on a mix of strong and weak foundations, our understanding of ourselves and the world around us can be based on a blend of empowering and limiting worldviews. Individuals can unite a Growth Mindset in their professional lives, embracing challenges and seeing failures as learning opportunities while simultaneously succumbing to a Fear-Driven mentality in their relationships, avoiding risks and potential emotional discomfort.

These conflicting worldviews can coexist within us, each influencing different aspects of our lives. The danger lies in that we might not even be aware of these harmful worldviews or the damage they're causing. We might excel in one area of life while unknowingly sabotaging ourselves in another. Or we might believe we follow empowering worldviews when limiting perspectives subtly influence our actions and decisions.

This is why examining our worldviews critically and holistically is so essential. We must strive to uncover and bring these hidden perspectives into our conscious awareness. Only then can we start to understand their impact on our lives and begin the process of transforming them.

But how do we identify these harmful worldviews that lurk beneath our conscious awareness? One approach is to look for patterns in our thoughts, feelings, and behaviors that seem to hold us back or cause us distress. These patterns can be clues pointing toward underlying worldviews not serving us well.

For instance, if we notice that we're often anxious about the future, we might hold onto a Fear-Driven mentality. If we constantly compare our possessions to those of others, we might be trapped in the Hollow Pursuit of Materialism and Consumerism.

These patterns are only sometimes easy to spot and uncovering them can take time and effort. This is where self-reflection, mindfulness, and self-awareness come into play. These practices can help us tune into our internal experiences, recognize recurring patterns, and uncover the underlying worldviews that drive them.

Worldviews are the invisible lens through which we interpret our experiences, the filter that colors our perception of reality. They shape our understanding of ourselves, others, and the world. They influence our attitudes, our behaviors, and our relationships. They inform us about our ethics, our politics, and our spirituality. They guide our decision-making process and shape our response to life's challenges and opportunities.

Before we can confront and transform harmful worldviews, we first need to identify and define them. This step is crucial, as it equips us with the understanding required to challenge and change these perspectives. It's important to remember that worldviews are not fixed, no matter how entrenched they seem. They are moldable and can be reshaped with conscious effort and persistence.

As we navigate a swiftly changing world where technology relentlessly evolves, geographical borders become increasingly fluid, and social structures shift like sands in the wind, the importance of our worldviews in shaping our interaction with our environment is essential. Despite this, all worldviews are not created equal.

The first worldview we examine is the Fixed Mindset, a rigid perspective that effectively serves as a prison for your potential, restricting your dreams to the confines of its bars. This worldview views abilities and intelligence as set in stone, hindering growth, development, and the pursuit of personal excellence.

Next, we delve into the Fear-Driven mentality, a worldview that conjures an intimidating monster out of uncertainty, shackling you with chains of anxiety and apprehension. This perspective promotes avoidance over action, stifling innovation, courage, and the spirit of adventure.

Third, we tackle the Hollow Pursuit of Materialism and Consumerism, a deceptive mirage that lures you away from genuine satisfaction and fulfillment. This worldview measures worth through material accumulation, leading to a never-ending cycle of acquisition that leaves little room for appreciation and contentment.

Fourth, we look at the Downward Spiral of Pessimism and Negativity, a vortex that siphons the joy and positivity from your life. This perspective encourages a focus on failures and setbacks, obscuring the view of possibilities and opportunities that lie ahead.

Lastly, we confront the Barrier of Ethnocentrism and Prejudice, a towering wall that isolates you from the rich, diverse tapestry of human cultures and experiences. This worldview instills a sense of superiority and discrimination, hampering empathy, understanding, and global unity.

In the upcoming chapters, we will dissect these harmful worldviews and provide practical tools and strategies to dismantle them, building healthier perspectives that foster growth, development, and fulfillment. We will guide you through cultivating a Growth Mindset, an outlook that sees challenges as opportunities for learning and effort as a pathway to mastery.

This exploration is not merely an intellectual exercise. It's a call to action, a rallying cry for every reader to look inward, challenge their assumptions, and embark on a transformative journey toward a more enlightened perspective on life. This is your opportunity to cast off the shackles of limiting worldviews, seize your life's reins, steer your ship toward the horizon of your highest potential, and shake this generational curse.

The process of transformation continues for us as individuals. The ripples of our transformation can extend beyond the confines of our own lives, influencing those around us and contributing to a broader societal change. As we transform our worldviews, we also set an example for others, inspiring them to embark on their journeys of self-discovery and transformation. This way, our efforts can contribute to a collective shift towards more compassionate, equitable, and sustainable worldviews.

And remember, the transformation of worldviews isn't a one-time event. It's a continuous process, a lifelong journey. As we grow and evolve, so do our perspectives. Our worldviews will continue to shift and develop in response to new experiences, knowledge, and insights. This dynamic nature of worldviews makes this journey so exciting and rewarding.

So strap in and prepare yourself for an adventure of self-discovery and personal growth. Together, we will brave the storms of opposing worldviews and chart a course toward a brighter, more empowered future. Let's begin this journey of a lifetime.

Chapter 2

Worldview a Fixed Mindset and its Limitations

The fixed mindset, which assumes that our capabilities, intelligence, and talents are unchangeable, stifles growth and prevents individuals from bettering themselves. For example, an actor with a fixed mindset might never try out for more challenging roles due to fear of judgment or failure, ultimately limiting their potential as a professional actor. Similarly, a talented athlete with a fixed mindset may reach a performance plateau because they believe they cannot improve or overcome their shortcomings. Individuals with a fixed mindset may be less likely to adapt to change or compromise, leading to tension and stagnation in their relationships with others, which can harm personal connections.

In family life, having a fixed mindset can result in rigid expectations and a lack of adaptability, causing friction and disconnection between family members. Individuals with a fixed mindset are less likely to realize their full professional potential, reducing their chances of success and career advancement. A fixed mindset can hinder an individual's spiritual growth and development by preventing them from exploring new beliefs, practices, or perspectives. This can inhibit them from expanding their spiritual horizons. When it comes to parenting, a fixed mindset can result in rigid expectations and an inability to adapt, hindering parents' ability to support their children's individual growth and development. Because children may internalize the belief that they cannot change or improve by adopting this mindset, it may discourage them from exploring new interests or taking on challenges.

Alex's Story:

My friend Alex, a bank teller for many years, discovered comfort in his life's regular and consistent patterns. Because of his knowledge and meticulous disposition, he had little trouble landing a specific profession in which he found fulfillment. He was the personification of a fixed mindset, a belief system his parents had implanted in him from an early age. According to this school of thought, intelligence, and talent are immutable characteristics that cannot be changed and are as reliable as the constellations in the night sky. This viewpoint handed down from generation to generation, established hidden links that kept the family within the boundaries of a self-limiting mentality.

Alex lived without the courage to walk into the unknown, learn from his failures, and develop his intrinsic potential. He was content with the life he had created for himself and was adamant in his conviction that there was no possible way to improve things. This perspective influenced all aspects of his life, including his familial ties, professional advancement, personal growth, and spiritual quest.

Alex's entrenched thinking was a glass ceiling that he created for himself in his professional life. He could not take on new tasks at work because his fear of failing and the possibility of facing ridicule in front of others paralyzed him. He did not venture out of his comfort zone and instead turned down challenging initiatives, which led to stagnation in his professional advancement. Consequently, he passed up much potential for personal and professional development.

His close personal relationships were also forced to bear the weight of his unyielding mentality. Alex struggled to wrap his head around the idea of change and was adamantly opposed to making any concessions. His patient and compassionate wife, Sarah, a shining example of patience and kindness, frequently prompted him to be more open to new experiences and ideas. Alex, on the other hand, did not waver in his conviction that he was unchangeable and unmovable in this viewpoint. This stubbornness on both sides resulted in frequent arguments inside their marriage, contributing to an undercurrent of tension that was difficult to ignore.

The inflexibility of Alex's ideas eventually took its toll on his spirituality. He was so sure that his spiritual fate was predetermined and could not be changed that he prevented himself from investigating new spiritual pathways, practices, or beliefs. Consequently, he did not have a profound connection with God, which is an essential component of the existence of humans. His spiritual development came to a standstill, and he could not experience the inner serenity and tranquility potentially associated with spiritual growth.

Lisa and Tommy, his children, were not spared the repercussions that resulted from their father's refusal to bend. Regarding their academic achievement and extracurricular activities, Alex urged them to refrain from challenging themselves by expanding their horizons or going beyond the confines of their comfort zones. Alex had the misguided belief that Lisa's creative abilities were unimportant and unchangeable, so he suggested that she devote her attention to the study of mathematics and science instead. Because Tommy's father believed that his son's abilities couldn't be improved, the young athlete did not receive the respect from his father that he deserved for his athletic prowess. Because of his unyielding perspective, Alex's ties with his family have strained over time.

The strain within the family became increasingly apparent. Sarah had an increasingly difficult time reconciling her beliefs with her husband, who resisted growth and change. Because of the limitations imposed on them by their father's expectations, Lisa and Tommy started to turn away from him and seek other sources of support and motivation.

Alex's life was forever changed when he was passed up for a promotion at his place of employment. This was a defining moment for Alex. He had to admit the limitations of his fixed thinking because he could not understand the cause of his exclusion. As he thought about his life, he concluded that his inflexible point of view had impeded him in various aspects, including professionally, personally, and spiritually.

The life of Alex is a glaring example of the dangers that might result from having a fixed worldview. Because he refused to acknowledge that he could develop and change, he could not take advantage of certain professional chances, his relationships were more strained, and his spiritual development was stunted. The two challenges are the self-awareness to recognize these problems and the fortitude to do something about them. Even when Alex began to rethink his long-held convictions, the path to transformation seemed difficult and daunting to him.

How do social media, films, and television influence this fixed mindset worldview?

Social media can perpetuate the notion that a person's abilities are static and unchangeable. For instance, social media platforms often showcase the highlights of people's lives, which can create an unrealistic benchmark for success and accomplishment. This portrayal can lead individuals to believe they cannot achieve the same level of success as others, fostering a fixed mindset. Films and television shows can also contribute to fixed mindset beliefs by disseminating negative stereotypes and promoting unrealistic standards of achievement and happiness.

Movies and television series may depict characters with fixed mindsets as successful, reinforcing the misconception that intelligence and talent are innate and immutable traits. Social media platforms can further exacerbate this belief by presenting curated images of individuals' lives and accomplishments, suggesting that success and talent are inborn and unattainable for others. For example, numerous movies and TV shows feature characters who display fixed mindsets or storylines that perpetuate fixed mindset beliefs, such as:

The Social Network (2010): This film about the creation of Facebook portrays Mark Zuckerberg as an innately talented individual whose success is primarily due to his inherent abilities rather than hard work and perseverance.

The Big Bang Theory (TV Series, 2007–2019): This sitcom frequently portrays its main characters, particularly Sheldon Cooper, as inherently intelligent and successful in their fields, without acknowledging the hard work, learning, and growth that contributed to their success.

Good Will Hunting (1997): The film revolves around a janitor at the Massachusetts Institute of Technology (MIT) who is a self-taught genius. The storyline emphasizes his innate intelligence, downplaying the role of effort and practice in his success.

Little Miss Sunshine (2006): The movie tells the story of a dysfunctional family on a road trip to support their daughter, who dreams of winning a beauty pageant. The film perpetuates the idea that physical beauty is an innate and unchangeable trait.

Glee (TV Series, 2009–2015): The show often focuses on the idea that some individuals are born with natural talent and are destined for success, while others will always struggle, reinforcing fixed mindset beliefs.

A Beautiful Mind (2001): This biographical drama about John Nash, a brilliant mathematician with schizophrenia, emphasizes Nash's innate genius and downplays the role of perseverance and hard work in his achievements.

These examples illustrate how social media, films, and television can influence and perpetuate fixed mindset beliefs, impacting individuals' perceptions of their abilities and potential for growth.

How can you tell if you might be subject to fixed mindset chains that are invisible to the naked eye?

Resistance to feedback:
If you take constructive criticism personally rather than as a chance to improve.

Comparing yourself to others:
Instead of developing yourself, you compare yourself to others.

Avoiding new experiences:
Trying new things, learning new skills, or leaving your comfort zone will show your weaknesses.

Attributing success to luck or external factors:
Instead of acknowledging your growth and hard work, you credit luck, circumstances, or others.

Blaming others or circumstances:
You blame others instead of learning from your mistakes.

Believing talent alone leads to success:
If you think success depends on talent rather than effort or learning.

Giving up easily:
You'll give up quickly if you think you can't overcome obstacles.

Let's talk about the other worldview now, the one that keeps people frozen in fear.

Chapter 3

Worldviews that drive Fear-Driven mentality

A worldview can drive fear in several ways. One way is by shaping how we perceive and interpret the world. Our beliefs and values can color how we interpret events and situations, and if our worldview emphasizes a sense of danger or threat, we may be more likely to feel afraid or anxious. For example, suppose someone holds a worldview that emphasizes a sense of scarcity or competition for resources. In that case, they may feel anxious or fearful about losing their job or being unable to provide for their family.

Similarly, suppose someone holds a worldview that demonizes certain groups of people as dangerous or threatening. In that case, they may feel afraid or distrustful of those groups even if they have no direct experience or evidence of harm. Another way a worldview can drive fear is by reinforcing certain behaviors or attitudes, perpetuating a cycle of anxiety or insecurity. For example, suppose someone's worldview emphasizes the importance of obedience and conformity to authority figures. In that case, they may fear breaking the rules or questioning authority, even if doing so might be in their best interest.

Ultimately, our worldview shapes our perceptions, beliefs, and behaviors and can significantly influence how we experience and respond to fear. By understanding the underlying beliefs and values that drive our fears, we can work to shift our worldview toward one that promotes courage, compassion, and resilience.

Additionally, a worldview can drive fear by creating a sense of "us vs. them" or an "enemy mentality." When we view the world in terms of black and white or in terms of friend or foe, it can create a sense of fear and anxiety toward those we perceive as different or unfamiliar. For example, suppose someone holds a worldview that prioritizes nationalism and sees other countries or cultures as a threat.

In that case, they may feel fearful or hostile towards people from those cultures, even if they have had no personal experience with or interaction with them. Similarly, if someone's worldview is based on a rigid set of religious or moral beliefs, they may view people who don't adhere to those beliefs as a threat or danger, leading to feelings of fear and mistrust.

A fear-driven mindset concentrates on potential threats, risks, and unfavorable outcomes, which can cause anxiety and self-doubt. Those with an entrepreneurial mindset driven by fear may never launch their innovative product because the worry paralyzes them, fearing they will fail or be rejected. This stifling mentality can also prevent famous and wealthy people from being able to appreciate their achievements. They are constantly concerned that they will lose their fame or fortune, which causes them to live a life fraught with tension and unhappiness.

In addition, individuals driven by fear may find it challenging to develop meaningful relationships. Their persistent anxiety may cause them to engage in excessive self-protection and be emotionally unavailable to others. A fear-driven mindset concentrates on potential threats, risks, and unfavorable outcomes, which can cause anxiety and self-doubt.

A worldview mindset that is motivated by fear has the potential to produce an anxious and overprotective atmosphere within families, which may stifle the members' capacity for personal development and independence.

As a result, these individuals may avoid engaging with their spirituality or exploring their faith. This way of thinking can lead to a parenting style that is overprotective, which has the potential to stunt children's development and independence. Fear-driven parents may unintentionally share their anxieties with their kids, making them hesitant to take chances or pursue their interests and passions.

Finally, our worldview can drive fear by reinforcing negative stereotypes or beliefs about ourselves or our abilities. We may fear taking risks or pursuing our goals if we hold a worldview emphasizing our flaws or limitations. For example, if someone holds a worldview that they are not intelligent or capable, they may fear challenging themselves or seeking new opportunities. Similarly, someone with a worldview that they are not attractive or desirable may fear rejection or judgment from others.

In conclusion, how we understand the world affects how we react to frightening situations. We can work to change our worldview toward one that encourages development, resilience, and agency by recognizing and analyzing the beliefs and values that contribute to our fears. Now let's dive into Amelia's backstory, knowing that a fear-based worldview can hinder you from having a healthy life.

Amelia's Story:

I was introduced to an intriguing woman named Amelia in the lively downtown of Omaha, Nebraska. The seminar was about how to launch a startup, and it was there that I met Amelia. Our connection grew stronger after we found out that we both had comparable concerns regarding the beginning of our business. This friend was responsible for bringing us together. While Amelia aspired to launch her clothing line, I had ambitions of opening a children's clothing store called New York City Kids in Omaha, Nebraska. The store would be in the busy Oakview Mall.

As my acquaintance with Amelia deepened, I became aware of her fear-based mentality's profound effect on every aspect of her existence. Amelia was unable to pursue her passion because of her fear-dominated mindset. She was constantly anxious about the possible outcomes and consequences of her actions, which caused her to become immobilized and unable to take the first step. This way of thinking interfered with her aspirations for her career and spread to every other area of her life.

Amelia's fear-driven mindset made her overly cautious and unwilling to take chances or try out novel things in her family life. Because of her worries and fears, she struggled to develop meaningful relationships with her family members. This caused her to be emotionally distant from them. Her worry about hurting the people she cared about most only drove them further away, leaving her with a sense of alienation and loneliness. Amelia's fear-driven mindset also had an impact on her career. Even though she was talented and dedicated, her persistent focus on possible dangers and unfavorable outcomes prevented her from taking chances or volunteering for difficult projects.

Because of this, she could not leave a job that wasn't giving her what she needed, which made her anxious and even more unhappy. Amelia had a deep yearning, on a spiritual level, to find more meaning and purpose in her life. Still, she could not investigate her spirituality or get involved with her faith. She could not find the comfort and guidance she desperately needed because of her fear of the unknown and other people's opinions. Her fear-driven mentality hurt her relationships with her friends as well.

Because of her anxiety, Amelia became guarded and reluctant to open up to other people, which decreased the depth of her relationships. Amelia's friends frequently thought that they were on the outside looking in as they struggled to comprehend her and form a more meaningful connection with her. Amelia's fear-based mentality during her formative years helped shape how she approaches parenting today. She had a hard time balancing her desire to shield her children from harm with her desire to let them experience life and learn from it on their terms.

Because of her persistent anxiety and nervousness, she became overbearingly controlling and stifling, stunting her children's growth and development. Amelia eventually overcame her fear of the unknown and had a prosperous career as a nurse. She did not allow her anxiety to prevent her from achieving the next step in her life's journey. She solemnly swore that she would never again allow fear to prevent her from achieving her goals, just as it had previously prevented her from opening a children's clothing store. Amelia's dogged determination motivated me; consequently, I overcame my anxiety and eventually achieved my goal of pursuing a career in information technology and leadership. But that's a tale for another time and place.

How do social media, films, and television influence this fear-driven worldview?

It all started with sensationalism, where news and media outlets focused on negative events, crime, and disasters to draw attention. This created a skewed perception of reality, making people believe the world was much more dangerous than it was. As people continued to scroll through their social media feeds, they found themselves in echo chambers, only exposed to content aligned with their interests and beliefs. This selective exposure reinforced their existing fears and anxieties, making them more susceptible to feeling afraid.

Films and television shows also played a part, using fear to engage viewers with dramatic or suspenseful storylines. These stories exploited common fears and anxieties, normalizing a fear-driven mindset and making it a daily life. Misinformation and fake news spread like wildfire on social media platforms, exacerbating fear and panic. Without proper fact-checking, people believed false narratives that contributed to their fearful worldview. Amidst all this, the constant exposure to violent or fear-inducing content desensitized people to real-world issues, creating a sense of apathy or indifference. This desensitization led to the normalization of fear as a default emotion when confronted with uncertainty.

Moreover, the media perpetuated stereotypes, stigmatizing certain groups, cultures, or situations. This further contributed to a fear-driven mindset, as people saw "others" as potential threats rather than appreciating the diversity and nuances of different people and situations. In this digital age, to counteract the influence of social media, films, and television on their fear-driven mindset, people learned the importance of consuming diverse content, practicing critical thinking, and engaging in open-minded discussions with others. They also found solace in taking breaks from media consumption and focusing on positive aspects of life, helping them break free from the grip of fear-based narratives.

For example, numerous movies and TV shows feature characters who display fixed mindsets or storylines that perpetuate fixed mindset beliefs, such as:

Black Mirror (2011): This anthology series often features characters with fear-driven mindsets as it explores technology's dark and dystopian consequences. Many episodes delve into the paranoia and fear that can arise from an over-reliance on technology, which can also perpetuate a fixed mindset.

Jaws (1975): The classic thriller about a great white shark terrorizing a coastal town portrays a fear-driven mindset in the characters and the storyline. The fear of the shark affects not only the townspeople but also the authorities, leading to irrational and dangerous actions.

War of the Worlds (2005): This sci-fi film, based on H.G. Wells' novel, depicts an alien invasion and the ensuing fear-driven mindset of the human population. The story highlights how fear can drive people to extremes, even leading them to betray one another in the struggle for survival.

Paranormal Activity (2007): This horror film series plays on common fears, such as the fear of the unknown, supernatural entities, and losing control. The fear-driven mindsets of the characters lead them to make choices that often exacerbate their situation, demonstrating how fear can cloud judgment.

The Purge (2013): This dystopian film series is set in a society that allows all crimes, including murder, to be legal for one night each year. The fear-driven mindset of the characters leads to chaos and violence, as people act on their worst instincts and take advantage of the lawlessness.

The popular TV show The Walking Dead (2010-2022): follows a group of survivors trying to survive in a zombie-infested post-apocalyptic world. The fear of zombies and other hostile human groups drives the characters to make choices based on survival and self-preservation, often leading to morally ambiguous decisions.

These movies and TV shows demonstrate the power of fear-driven mindsets and fixed beliefs in shaping the actions and decisions of characters, often leading to negative outcomes.

However, there are signs and behaviors you can look for that may indicate the presence of a fear-driven mindset.

Excessive worry and anxiety:
Fear-driven mindsets involve worrying about worst-case scenarios, potential dangers, and negative outcomes, even with no evidence to support them.

Avoidance behavior:
Fear-driven people avoid situations, people, and experiences. Avoiding social situations out of fear of judgment or rejection may limit your experience and opportunities.

Over-reliance on safety behaviors:
Fear-driven people use rituals, habits, or coping mechanisms to feel safe or in control. Safety behaviors can be adaptive, but overuse can stifle growth and maintain fear.

Difficulty making decisions:
Fear-driven mindsets make it hard to make decisions or act. Indecision, procrastination, and missed opportunities can result.

Overgeneralization:
A fear-driven mindset may cause you to apply a negative experience or fear to unrelated situations. If you had a bad dog experience and now avoid all dogs, even friendly ones, you may overgeneralize your fear.

Perfectionism:
A fear-driven mindset may cause you to obsess over perfection and avoid mistakes. Perfectionism can hinder growth and well-being due to a fear of failure, rejection, or criticism.

Let's discuss the third worldview, the empty pursuit of materialism and consumerism. It has the most significant influence out of the five because of how many people buy into it.

Chapter 4

The Hollow Pursuit of Materialism and Consumerism

A materialistic and consumer-driven worldview prioritizes material wealth, possessions, and external validation over personal growth, relationships, and self-discovery. This mindset can strain family relationships, as pursuing material success may overshadow the importance of emotional connection and support. In careers, a materialistic focus can lead to dissatisfaction and burnout, as individuals may prioritize financial gain over personal fulfillment and work-life balance. Spiritually, materialism and consumerism can detract from pursuing inner peace and meaning, as individuals may seek external validation rather than develop a deeper connection with their spirituality.

This mindset can negatively impact parenting by encouraging a focus on material success and achievement rather than emotional connection and support. Children raised in such an environment may develop a superficial understanding of success and happiness, neglecting the importance of personal growth, relationships, and inner fulfillment.

Materialism and consumerism are pervasive in contemporary society, particularly within affluent nations. In these societies, individuals often find themselves caught in a cycle of acquiring and consuming goods and services that extend well beyond their basic needs.

In this environment, the media and advertising play significant roles. They present material goods as the keys to happiness and success, fostering an insatiable desire for more. However, reality often needs to catch up to these promised ideals. The happiness derived from acquiring new possessions tends to be short-lived, leading to a seemingly endless cycle of desire and disappointment.

The psychological impact of this pursuit can be profound. Studies suggest that those prioritizing material wealth experience lower well-being and satisfaction in life. They are also more likely to suffer from anxiety and depression, indicating that pursuing material wealth does not deliver the fulfillment it promises.

The pursuit of material goods can also affect interpersonal connections. People risk becoming socially isolated and dissatisfied when they place more value on their worldly belongings than their interpersonal relationships. These relationships are prone to being superficial and unsatisfying, further contributing to a feeling of emptiness.

The following is an excerpt from a comment made by Steve Jobs near the end of his life: "You will realize your true inner happiness does not come from the material things of this world. If the plane crashes, you will go down in first class or economy. There is no escape. Therefore. I hope you know that true happiness is achieved when you have mates, buddies, and old friends, brothers, and sisters, whom you can chat with, laugh with, talk with, sing songs with, and talk about where the north, south, east, and west are located, or heaven and earth."

The following two tales demonstrate how a worldview's emphasis on consumerism and materialism shapes a person's worldview and subsequent actions.

Steven's Story:

A friend of mine named Steven was raised with materialism and material wealth as the ultimate objectives of life. While he was growing up in a social media, television, and film-filled environment, his parents repeatedly told him that success was equivalent to material prosperity and professional status. Steven, a youth from the middle class, became mesmerized by media depictions of lavish lifestyles. As a result, he began to believe he merited such extravagance and failed to appreciate the effort required to achieve such a position.

At 18 years old, Steven received his first credit card, an American Express card, even though he didn't have a job. This event profoundly impacted his life. Misformation about the true value of money, Steven was easily led astray by the lures financial institutions set for young people. The lure of quick credit and the desire to be like the TV characters he saw fueled his descent into materialistic excess. He accumulated significant debt and indulged in extravagant vacations, posh hotels, and expensive restaurants. However, this glitzy facade could only be maintained for a while.

Soon, Steven was forced to face the harsh realities of his situation, which manifested as mounting credit card debt. The invisible restraints of materialism and consumerism began to weigh heavily on him, eventually leading to depression and a feeling that his life lacked value. Unaware of the danger in the worldviews he was teaching his children, he perpetuated the generational curse.

Social media and mainstream entertainment often gloss over the notion that achieving success requires effort and dedication. As a result, many young adults like Steven seek instant gratification, which can lead to harmful addictions and illegal activities. The pressure to maintain a wealthy lifestyle eventually becomes unbearable, exacerbating the negative impacts caused by materialism and consumerism.

Not only did Steven's struggles with materialism and consumerism detrimentally affect his finances, but they also severely impacted his relationships and friendships. Platforms like Facebook, TikTok, and YouTube encourage users to chase fame and money, contributing to society's wealth and power aspirations in the modern era. However, there is hope. Individuals like Steven can break free from their shackles, make better decisions, and ultimately find happiness beyond the superficial trappings of wealth and success by being aware of the perils of materialism and consumerism. This book will explore the liberation from these unseen chains.

Lisa's Story:

Lisa was born and raised in Kansas City, Missouri, in the 1980s. As a young, poor Hispanic woman at 21, she immersed herself in a culture prioritizing wealth and material possessions above all else. The impact of consumerism and materialism on her life profoundly shaped her worldview. It influenced her decisions as she transitioned from a young adult into a wife, mother, and career woman.

Growing up, Lisa was exposed to a constant barrage of advertising and media messages that equated success with owning the latest gadgets, wearing designer clothes, and driving luxury cars. As a result, she began to internalize these values, feeling that she needed to acquire material possessions to be happy and successful.

As Lisa grew older, her fixation on consumerism and materialism affected her relationships, career, and spirituality. When she met her husband, their shared interest in material goods initially seemed like a bonding factor. However, as they started a family together, the focus on wealth and material possessions strained their marriage.

As Lisa and her husband tried to keep up with the Joneses, they found themselves working long hours and neglecting their relationship and children in the pursuit of material wealth. Their priorities became increasingly misaligned with their true values, and the stress of maintaining a facade of affluence began to take a toll on their emotional well-being and family life.

Lisa's focus on material success in her career led her to prioritize promotions and financial gain over job satisfaction and personal fulfillment. While she could climb the corporate ladder, she felt empty and unfulfilled, as her work needed more meaning and purpose.

Lisa's obsession with materialism and consumerism similarly stunted her spiritual development. As she focused on accumulating wealth and possessions, she neglected her inner self and the cultivation of a spiritual practice. This left her disconnected from her true self and life's larger purpose.

As the years went by, the impact of consumerism and materialism on Lisa's life became increasingly apparent. Her marriage suffered, her children felt neglected, and her career, though financially successful, left her feeling unfulfilled. The once-shared values that had brought her and her husband together now seemed to be driving them apart, and the superficial trappings of success failed to provide the happiness and contentment they had sought.

Lisa's story is a cautionary tale, illustrating the detrimental effects of a worldview focused on consumerism and materialism. By prioritizing wealth and possessions above all else, she compromised her relationships, career, and spiritual growth, ultimately finding that pursuing material success brought her neither happiness nor fulfillment. However, there is hoped to recognize these unseen chains, and this book will serve as a guide to identify the worldviews and steps to break free.

How do social media, films, and television influence this Consumerism and Materialism worldview?

The rise of social media, films, and television has given birth to an era where information is readily available at our fingertips. This global interconnectedness has undeniably had its advantages but has also facilitated the spread of consumerism and materialism. Let's explore how these platforms affect career, family, friends, parenting, and spirituality, exploring the negative consequences of a consumerist and materialistic worldview.

This worldview has a powerful impact on career choices, as it often portrays high-paying jobs and lavish lifestyles as the epitome of success. Consequently, many individuals are driven to pursue careers that promise wealth and status, regardless of their passion, skills, or interests. This misalignment between personal values and career choices can result in job dissatisfaction, burnout, and high rates of job-hopping.

Additionally, social media platforms have made it easy for users to compare their achievements with their peers, fueling the "comparison trap." This constant comparison can lead to feelings of inadequacy, jealousy, and a never-ending pursuit of material success. In extreme cases, this pressure can lead to mental health issues such as anxiety, depression, and a pervasive sense of failure. People struggle to keep up with the unrealistic standards set by media portrayals.

The culture of consumerism and materialism propagated by social media, films, and television has profoundly impacted relationships. The relentless pursuit of material possessions can cause people to become more self-centered and less empathetic, making it difficult to maintain deep, meaningful connections with family and friends.

Relationships can become transactional, as individuals are more likely to value others based on their material possessions or social status than their character or emotional connection. Moreover, the competitive nature of consumerism can lead to envy, jealousy, and resentment among friends and family members. This unhealthy competition can damage relationships, as people may become more focused on outdoing one another rather than nurturing and supporting each other.

The portrayal of parenting in social media, films, and television often revolves around providing children with the latest gadgets, fashionable clothes, and extravagant experiences. Parents may feel pressured to keep up with these trends to appease their children and maintain an image of being "good" parents among their peers. This emphasis on material possessions can overshadow the importance of teaching children essential life skills, emotional intelligence, and resilience.

Furthermore, the materialistic mindset may lead children to develop a sense of entitlement and an unhealthy dependence on material goods for happiness and self-worth. In the long run, this can result in adults struggling with emotional well-being, social relationships, and finding meaning and purpose in life.

This worldview can have a detrimental impact on one's spiritual growth. Focusing on material possessions and external validation can distract individuals from seeking deeper meaning, purpose, and connection. As a result, people may experience a sense of emptiness and discontent, even when they have seemingly achieved material success.

Many spiritual traditions emphasize the importance of self-reflection, humility, and detachment from material possessions. However, the consumerist culture encourages a superficial, self-centered approach to life, often incompatible with these spiritual principles. This incongruity can leave individuals feeling disconnected from their spiritual roots and struggling to find inner peace.

Ultimately, everyone is responsible for recognizing the impact of consumerism and materialism on their lives and making conscious choices that prioritize long-term happiness, personal growth, and the well-being of others. By doing so, we can create a future where success is measured not by what we own but by who we are and our positive impact on the world. However, it's a journey; we will explore it more through this book.

Numerous movies and TV shows feature characters who display consumerism and materialism, often glamorizing these values and influencing the behavior and attitudes of viewers. **Some notable examples include:**

The Wolf of Wall Street (2013): This film, based on the true story of Jordan Belfort, portrays a stockbroker's relentless pursuit of wealth, power, and material possessions, emphasizing the excesses and corruption that can accompany such a lifestyle.

Sex and the City (1998–2004): This popular TV series follows the lives of four women in New York City, often showcasing their luxurious lifestyles, designer clothes, and expensive shoes, reinforcing the importance of material possessions and social status.

The Great Gatsby (2013): Based on F. Scott Fitzgerald's classic novel, this film depicts the opulent, extravagant lifestyle of the wealthy during the Roaring Twenties. The protagonist, Jay Gatsby, is obsessed with material possessions in his quest to win back the love of his life.

Keeping Up with the Kardashians (2007-2021): This reality TV show revolves around the lives of the Kardashian-Jenner family, who are known for their luxurious lifestyles, designer wardrobes, and extravagant vacations. The show has been criticized for promoting materialism and consumerism.

Crazy Rich Asians (2018): This romantic comedy showcases the ultra-wealthy lifestyle of Singapore's elite, emphasizing the importance of luxury goods, opulent homes, and extravagant parties in their lives.

These examples demonstrate the pervasive presence of consumerism and materialism in movies and TV shows. These portrayals can influence viewers' perceptions of what constitutes a successful and fulfilling life, potentially leading to negative consequences in various aspects of their lives, such as careers, relationships, parenting, and spirituality.

Several signs and behaviors may indicate the presence of a consumerism and materialism mindset in an individual. Awareness of these signs can help recognize and address these values, promoting a more balanced and fulfilling lifestyle. Some of these signs and behaviors include:

Constant comparison:
Individuals with a materialistic mindset may constantly compare their possessions, lifestyle, and achievements with others, leading to envy, jealousy, and dissatisfaction.

Excessive spending:
A strong focus on acquiring material goods may result in excessive spending, leading to financial strain, debt, and an inability to save for the future.

Defining success by possessions:
Those with a consumerist mentality often measure their success and self-worth by the quantity and quality of their material possessions rather than their personal growth, relationships, or spiritual well-being.

Obsession with brands and status symbols:
A materialistic individual may place significant importance on owning designer labels, luxury items, and status symbols, believing these items will enhance their social standing and personal image.

Neglecting relationships and personal growth:
A preoccupation with material possessions and consumerism may lead to neglecting interpersonal relationships, personal development, and spiritual growth, as these aspects of life are prioritized over acquiring material goods.

Short-term happiness:
Those with a consumerist mindset may derive happiness from acquiring new material possessions. Still, this sense of satisfaction is often short-lived, leading to a constant cycle of wanting and acquiring more.

Lack of gratitude and contentment:
Materialistic individuals may struggle to feel gratitude and contentment with what they have as they continually focus on what they lack or desire.

Prioritizing material goods over experiences:
Individuals with a materialistic mindset might prioritize acquiring material possessions overspending on experiences, such as travel, personal development courses, or social activities, which can contribute to overall well-being and happiness.

Now on to the fourth worldview, The Downward Spiral of Pessimism and Negativity.

Chapter 5

The Downward Spiral of Pessimism and Negativity

This way of looking at the world can lead to actions and results that aren't very productive, which can then make the situation even worse, resulting in a vicious cycle. Pessimism and negativity can hurt a person's performance at work and hinder their ability to advance professionally. A person with this point of view might be more likely to dwell on their shortcomings rather than their accomplishments and be more likely to be unduly critical of their skills. This can lead to a drop in motivation, leading to lower productivity and less interaction with coworkers.

In addition, a pessimistic outlook may make it more difficult to succeed in one's profession, given that employers frequently place a premium on individuals with both an optimistic outlook and good problem-solving abilities. A pessimistic attitude can put a strain on personal relationships and cause damage to them. When someone continually dwells on the unfavorable elements of life, it can be challenging for friends and family members to establish a relationship with that individual. This can result in the individual becoming socially isolated since they may become less eager to participate in social activities or have meaningful conversations with others. Over time, this can cause strained relationships or lead to the complete disintegration of friendships and familial ties.

Pessimism and negativity may impede a person's capacity for spiritual growth and development. When one has a pessimistic outlook on the world, finding meaning and purpose in one's life and keeping a grateful attitude toward one's experiences can be difficult. People with a pessimistic outlook may be more likely to experience hopelessness and despair, hindering their ability to connect with a higher power or explore their spiritual beliefs. People with a pessimistic outlook may be more likely to experience helplessness and despair. In conclusion, the downward spiral of pessimism and negativity can have far-reaching effects on an individual's career path, relationships, and spiritual development.

Tim's Story:

Tim was a talented individual with a wealth of experience in the tech industry. He had worked at several prestigious companies, building applications and solving complex problems. However, a persistent cloud of pessimism and negativity clouded Tim's outlook on life. Tim was married to a loving and supportive wife, Jane, and together they had two children, a 10-year-old son named Sam and a 7-year-old daughter named Lucy. But his negative worldview impacted every aspect of his life, including his family and career.

At work, Tim was constantly anxious about his projects, worried that they would fail or that he would make a mistake. His pessimistic attitude affected his professional relationships, causing him to become increasingly isolated from his colleagues. He missed out on opportunities for career advancement, as his employers saw him as someone who focused more on problems than solutions. His negativity seeped into his marriage as well. Tim often came home stressed and overwhelmed, sharing only his work challenges with his wife. Jane tried her best to encourage and support him, but the constant negativity took a toll on their relationship.

Tim's pessimistic outlook also affected his relationship with his children. Tim unwittingly focused on their shortcomings and difficulties instead of celebrating their accomplishments and nurturing their interests. Sam and Lucy felt the weight of their father's negativity and began to doubt their abilities. Tim's friendships suffered as well. He became less inclined to participate in social activities or meaningful conversations with friends. Eventually, he grew distant from his closest friend, Sarah, and others who cared about him. His social circle shrank, and he found himself feeling lonely and isolated.

Additionally, Tim's pessimistic worldview also had an impact on his spiritual life. He struggled to find meaning and purpose in his existence, questioning the point of his hard work and accomplishments. His sense of spirituality waned, and he felt disconnected from any sense of a higher power or a greater purpose.

Tim's life spiraled downward, his career stalled, his marriage strained, and his relationship with his children weakened. His friendships dwindled, and his spiritual growth was stunted. Despite his talent and potential, Tim's pessimism and negativity clouded his ability to see the positive aspects of his life, leading to a series of non-productive outcomes and deep dissatisfaction. Tim's once-promising life seemed to unravel as the days turned into months. His work performance continued to suffer, and he started to receive negative feedback from his supervisors. They expressed concern about his attitude and lack of collaboration, warning that his job could be in jeopardy if he didn't make some changes.

At home, the atmosphere became increasingly tense. Jane found herself shouldering the emotional burden of their family, trying to maintain a positive environment for their children while also dealing with her own feelings of frustration and sadness. The couple's once-strong connection began to fray, and they argued more frequently.

Sensing the growing tension at home, Sam and Lucy became more withdrawn and anxious. Their father's constant focus on the negative made them struggle with schoolwork and friendships, undermining their confidence in their abilities. One evening, after another heated argument, Tim found himself alone in his home office, reflecting on the wreckage his negativity had brought to his life.

His once-thriving career was on the brink of collapse, his marriage was in crisis, and he was losing touch with his children. His friends had disappeared, and he felt a profound emptiness where his spiritual life used to be. In that moment of painful self-awareness, Tim realized he needed to change. He knew continuing this path of pessimism and negativity would only lead to more heartache and disappointment. Tim resolved to break the cycle and find a way to bring positivity and hope back into his life for his own sake and his family's.

How do social media, films, and television influence this Pessimism and Negativity worldview?

Social media, movies, and television can substantially impact an individual's worldview, contributing to the formation of pessimism and negativity and their further spread. The following are some examples of how exposure to these media sources can contribute to a pessimistic mindset. The highlights of people's lives are frequently showcased on social media, which might lead to an inaccurate picture of reality because these highlights are generally skillfully controlled. When one compares their own life to the lives of others who appear to have it all together, it can lead to emotions of inadequacy, jealousy, and self-doubt, which in turn can reinforce a gloomy outlook.

People are only exposed to material that validates their preexisting biases since the algorithms used by social media platforms are designed to show users content aligned with their interests and beliefs. This results in the establishment of echo chambers. This can perpetuate a pessimistic worldview by limiting exposure to more positive or balanced points of view and reinforcing pessimistic attitudes. To draw in viewers, movies and television shows frequently put drama, conflict, and controversy front and center.

This can cause a person to place undue importance on unfavorable occurrences and circumstances, distorting their view of reality and helping them develop a pessimistic worldview.

Films and television shows with violent or dismal themes might lead to a pessimistic outlook because they normalize violent behavior, portray hopeless futures, and emphasize the most unpleasant parts of people. The spectator may feel depressed and miserable about the world's state.

The news cycle that runs twenty-four hours a day tends to concentrate on unfavorable occurrences, such as crimes, natural catastrophes, and political disputes; this can result in an exaggerated feeling of fear and pessimism. In addition, receiving a steady diet of depressing news can cause a condition known as "mean world syndrome," in which a person develops the false impression that the world is significantly more dangerous and unfriendly than it is.

Media intake can reinforce cognitive biases, such as the negativity bias, which tends to attach more weight to unpleasant experiences than positive ones. Constant exposure to harmful content may exacerbate this bias, making it more challenging for people to appreciate the positive aspects of their lives and the world around them. Emotions can transfer from one person to another, and exposing oneself to pessimistic or unpleasant content might contribute to this phenomenon. When people consume media that causes them to feel unhappy, they may be more likely to share or create content that is emotionally like what they have experienced, which further contributes to the cycle of negativity.

Films and television shows frequently portray idealized depictions of romantic relationships, professional success, and happiness. This can lead audiences to have false expectations and a sense of dissatisfaction with their own lives. These depictions have the potential to cultivate a pessimistic mindset because they place emphasis on unreachable ideals and promote the understanding that living an average life is not sufficient. People may engage less in face-to-face social interactions as they spend more time-consuming content on various media platforms. Personal interactions are essential to mental health and can protect against detrimental influences. The decrease in the number of actual interpersonal connections may be one factor that contributes to an increasingly alienated and pessimistic mindset.

Numerous movies and TV shows feature characters who display pessimism and negativity, often glamorizing these values and influencing the behavior and attitudes of viewers. **Some notable examples include:**

Bojack Horseman (2014): He is a washed-up actor who suffers from depression, substance abuse, and self-pity, and he is portrayed in the Netflix series "Bojack Horseman" as Bojack. Bojack's pessimism and negativity are vital components of his persona, even though the program has received much praise for its accurate depiction of issues related to mental health.

Breaking Bad (2008): The lead character, Walter White, is initially likable. However, as the story progresses, White becomes more cynical, manipulative, and ethically compromised.

Squidward Tentacles from "SpongeBob SquarePants" (1999): Squidward is a noticeably negative character who frequently feels disappointed and depressed about his life under the sea. This is even though the show is geared for children.

Eeyore, a character from "Winnie the Pooh" (1988): Eeyore, although a character in a children's book and program, is recognized for his dismal, downbeat, and pessimistic attitude toward life. In

The Hitchhiker's Guide to the Galaxy (1981): The character Marvin the Paranoid Android says that Marvin, an android described as having "a brain the size of a planet," is always pessimistic and melancholy. He is well known for his negative view of virtually everything.

That '70s Show, character "Red Forman" (1998): Red, who plays the role of a strict father figure throughout the series, is frequently pessimistic and unpleasant, especially toward his son and the other people in his kid's life."

Oscar the Grouch (1969): Is a notably pessimistic character who appears on "Sesame Street." Oscar has chosen to live in a garbage can and has a disposition that is frequently grumpy.

These characters frequently provide comedic relief in the shows or movies in which they appear. Still, they also remind individuals that they might become socially isolated if they consistently express negative emotions. It is essential to remember that even if these characters exhibit pessimism and negativity, the television series and movies in which they appear typically do not glorify these characteristics. They are portrayed as complicated people who have flaws, and it is said that their bad attitudes frequently cause conflict and misery.

Several signs and behaviors may indicate the presence of pessimism and negativity in an individual. Awareness of these signs can help recognize and address these values, promoting a more balanced and fulfilling lifestyle. **Some of these signs and behaviors include:**

Negative self-talk:
It is a standard indicator of pessimism; pessimists frequently engage in it. This includes thinking and saying things that diminish one's value or ability, such as "I can't do this" or "I'm not good enough." The inclination to view any event in the most negative light is called "catastrophizing."

Chronically pessimistic people frequently prepare themselves for the worst and are persuaded that they are doomed to fail. Negative people tend to focus on the negative parts of a situation. Pessimistic people tend to concentrate on the negative details of a situation and miss the positive aspects. They tend to focus more on what went wrong than what went well. Pessimists tend to project their pessimism onto others, criticizing and insulting those around them or anticipating that the people they interact with will fail.

Absence of Motivation and Enthusiasm:
Pessimistic individuals may be unwilling to participate in things they formerly enjoyed or demonstrate apathy towards new experiences. Pessimists frequently prepare themselves for criticism and behave defensively in response to it. They may dismiss praise or favorable feedback because they believe the giver is not genuine.

Having a Pervasive Sense of Hopelessness Pessimism is often characterized by a pervasive hopelessness about the future. This might refer to something as specific as your professional life or personal connections, or it can refer to something as general as the status of the planet.

Negativism and pessimism that last for an extended period might put a person at risk of developing mental health problems such as chronic stress and depression. Complaining a lot and about a wide variety of topics simultaneously is one of the telltale signs of someone with a pessimistic worldview.

This may involve something as insignificant as a minor nuisance or something as significant as a major life catastrophe. Negativity and pessimism can strain relationships, making creating and maintaining strong connections with others challenging. This might make it more difficult to keep a positive attitude.

Let us continue our expedition into the next part of this barren landscape, where the pitfalls of this troublesome worldview await to be discovered: the shadowy realm of ethnocentrism and prejudice.

Chapter 6

The Barrier of Ethnocentrism and Prejudice

An ethnocentric and biased worldview casts long and destructive shadows, even though its supporters are frequently unaware of their blind spots. It's almost as if we're looking at the world through a keyhole, severely limiting our capacity to comprehend the intricate web of human history, civilizations, and experiences.

Ethnocentrism, in its most destructive form, blinds our eyes and causes us to believe that our culture, race, or nation is superior to that of other countries. It encourages a hierarchical structure in which some groups are considered more valuable than others, which is the fundamental cause of bias and discrimination. This worldview has the potential to foster social conflict, split communities, and rob people of the respect and chances to which they are entitled, just based on the cultural background or identity they were born into.

Another negative consequence of adopting such a limited point of view is the development of prejudice. It fosters prejudice and stereotyping, insinuating itself into our ideas, deeds, and choices without conscious awareness. This can perpetuate societal disparities and injustices, frequently putting marginalized groups in a worse position. People's life trajectories and possibilities can be radically altered due to prejudice permeating various facets of society, such as the workplace, the educational system, the housing market, and law enforcement.

An ethnocentric and biased attitude is also detrimental to one's personal development. It prevents us from having the enlightening experience of learning from the opinions and experiences of people from diverse cultures. Accepting variety may make our lives more fulfilling, it can encourage creativity and innovation, and it can lead to societies that are more harmonious and inclusive.

When we talk about a "generational curse," we refer to unfavorable habits, behaviors, or attitudes passed down from one generation to the next, typically in a subliminal manner. In this setting, ethnocentrism and prejudice can unquestionably serve the function of a curse; nevertheless, there are additional considerations that should also be taken into consideration.

Mismanagement of finances is a prevalent form of generational curse that can be traced back to poor financial habits. These behaviors can be passed down from generation to generation within a family, resulting in continued financial instability and stress if the family has a history of debt, overspending, or a lack of savings.

Abuse of substances Families with a tradition of substance abuse frequently observe the detrimental tendencies described above being carried on from generation to generation. Children brought up in such settings may accept these actions as typical, which can lead to a vicious cycle of addiction.

Habits that are Harmful to your health and Nutrition Unhealthy eating habits and sedentary lifestyles can be passed down from generation to generation, leading to health problems such as obesity, heart disease, and diabetes. Breaking these habits without conscious effort and instruction may be challenging because they are deeply imprinted.

Abuse and violence in the home can be learned behaviors passed down from generation to generation. When children are exposed to or experience domestic violence, they are at an increased risk of repeating these behaviors in their intimate partnerships later in life.

Refraining from focusing sufficiently on the significance of education can be a severe generational curse that results in poorer academic accomplishment and fewer opportunities for future careers. This loop can maintain socioeconomic inequities.

Patterns of Unhealthy Communication Unhealthy communication patterns, such as yelling, silent treatment, or emotional manipulation, can be passed down from generation to generation, harming relationships, and emotional health.

As a result, the hidden chains of an ethnocentric and biased worldview bind those subjected to it and limit the growth of those who harbor such ideas.

Lily's Story:

Lily was born in San Francisco to Chinese parents who came to the United States for a better life. She was a diligent student as a young girl and consistently ranked first in her class. Lily's mother, who had high expectations for her daughter, adhered to the stereotype of the "Asian Tiger Mom." She pushed Lily to thrive in all aspects of life, from academics to extracurricular activities, because she envisioned Lily having a successful and distinguished career as a physician or engineer.

On the other hand, Lily found herself lured by a different route. She had a deep-seated interest in teaching and had always imagined herself in that role. Her mother was surprised and disappointed when she revealed her goals to her. Her mother struggled to comprehend why Lily would pursue a career outside the high-status professions frequently linked with the stereotype of the "Model Minority." When she shared her goals, her mother was surprised and disappointed in her.

The amount of pressure coming from her mother was significant. To fulfill her mother's lofty expectations, Lily frequently found herself deep into her books well into the night, giving up her hobbies and spare time. She was always worried that she would let her mother down, which took a toll on her mental health and led to her experiencing stress, worry, and periods of insomnia. Her mother's mental health suffered as a result.

Lily faced the additional challenge of overcoming the "Perpetual Foreigner" reputation while she was in high school. Even though she was born and raised in the United States, her fellow students and professors frequently dealt with her as a foreigner. Lily experienced feelings of alienation and misunderstanding due to this, in addition to the pressure from her mother.

After finishing her education, she returned to her hometown to teach at the local high school. Upon her return, she realized that the stereotype of the "Model Minority" followed her everywhere. Many people were surprised by her decision to become a teacher because they assumed she would choose a profession more typically associated with prestige. Lily, on the other hand, was encouraged. She devoted herself to fostering a welcoming and encouraging atmosphere for students of all backgrounds in the classroom since she loved her job so much.

The trip that Lily took sheds light on the stress and emotional toll that individuals might experience due to the pressures and expectations placed on them by society. Lily disregarded her mother's and society's expectations and harmful prejudices to pursue her passion. She did this by fighting harmful stereotypes.

Jamal's Story:

A young man named Jamal is from the dynamic city of Atlanta, Georgia, in the state of Georgia. Although Jamal was the youngest of four siblings and came from a middle-class African American household, his parents strongly emphasized the value of education. However, for Jamal, their attention drifted toward the world of athletics. Jamal's innate athletic skills fascinated everyone around him from an early age, prompting his community to think that a future in athletics was ahead for him.

This is an all-too-prevalent stereotype that is pushed on young black men. Nevertheless, Jamal has a distinct fire within him. He was enamored with technology while the rest of his classmates were watching balls and medals, which sparked a strong desire to pursue a career in information technology. Jamal's years spent in high school have presented him with a difficult test of his mettle.

As he fought against the notion that people of African descent were not predisposed to flourish in academics, particularly in STEM subjects, he was met with a barrier of low expectations from both his teachers and peers. Mathematics, an essential topic for his chosen profession, became an extra obstacle to conquer. The suffocating weight of stereotypes did not deter Jamal, and he channeled his ambition accordingly. He actively sought additional guidance, conscientiously attended tutoring sessions, and devoted valuable time to mastering the challenging aspects of mathematics.

His abilities continued to improve with time, defying the expectations that could hinder his growth. Jamal would receive a harsh education, but fate had other plans. The piercing wail of police sirens disrupted the tranquility one unlucky day as he drove through the city streets in the gray Pontiac Grand Am that belonged to his mother. Jamal was given no warning before being pulled over, which resulted in a terrifying confrontation with law enforcement.

The infraction? An unjust accusation that targeted him exclusively since he is of a certain race was that he matched the description of a suspect involved in the theft of an automobile. Jamal's attempts to clarify the situation by stating that he was operating the vehicle that belonged to his mother were met with indifference. He was ordered out of the car, forcibly handcuffed, and humiliated as he sat on the curb; he was a victim of the ubiquitous "Criminal Stereotype" that plagued his neighborhood.

He felt unbearable embarrassment and helplessness as he went through these experiences. This act of racial profiling took place in broad daylight, in front of his classmates from school, who walked by in startled silence as they saw what had just happened. Jamal's sense of dignity was shattered as a direct result of the encounter, and it also served as a painful reminder of the subtle nature of racial bigotry. Because he had darker skin, he was picked out and made to endure unfair treatment.

This was not because of anything he had done in the past. Despite this, Jamal's soul remained unbroken despite the blazing embers of anguish and humiliation he endured. Instead of letting the event end his aspirations, he used it to motivate himself to continue his quest. He was burning from the inside out with a steely resolution. He directed his energy not just into attaining his dreams as an IT expert but also demolishing the harmful prejudices that afflicted his town.

He did this because these misconceptions tormented his community. The unconquerable path of Jamal serves as a powerful illustration of the transformative potential of resilience when confronted with challenging circumstances. His dogged pursuit of brilliance and his steadfast dedication to challenging the damaging narratives imposed upon him is a ray of light that points the way to a better future.

The media plays a vital role in forming our perspectives and attitudes, and it can potentially develop ethnocentrism and prejudice in various ways unintentionally. The adoption of stereotypes is one of the most typical and widespread methods by which this occurs. The media often exploits stereotypes as a shortcut to deliver information about people and circumstances quickly. However, when a specific group is often portrayed stereotypically, viewers can unintentionally embrace these stereotypes because of how the group is represented.

Adopting a biased way of thinking can lead to the formation of prejudices in an individual, some of which the individual may not even be aware of. Moreover, the representation of different ethnic, cultural, or social groups in media is frequently skewed. Some groups might be underrepresented or misrepresented, which can indirectly imply that these groups are less significant or even worse. This kind of representation, or the lack of it, can foster a sense of ethnocentrism in viewers who belong to the dominant group, reinforcing the notion that their culture is the norm or the standard.

This concept is further amplified by what's known as cultural imperialism. The majority of content in the media, particularly that which originates in Hollywood and other Western sources, tends to promote Western ideas, values, and lifestyles. Because of this dominance, viewers from different cultures may experience feelings of inferiority or marginalization, further reinforcing the ethnocentric views held by Western viewers. The impact of the media goes beyond the reporting of the news.

The press frequently pays disproportionate attention to unfavorable occurrences associated with racial, ethnic, or social groups. As a result, viewers may start associating these groups with destructive features or actions, establishing prejudiced attitudes. The echo chambers produced by social media platforms also play a significant role in developing an ethnocentric or prejudiced mindset. On these forums, people typically communicate with individuals who have similar ideas, strengthening their previous opinions and prejudices. This can lead to a lack of understanding and empathy for others outside of one's social or cultural group.

In addition, certain groups may be portrayed in the media as essentially distinct or on a lower level than humans, particularly in movies about conflict or crime. This kind of dehumanization can contribute to the perpetuation of prejudice and perhaps provoke hostility or violence toward the portrayed people. The media has the potential to normalize prejudice as well. It's typical for comedies, movies, or even content published online to make light of bias or discriminatory behavior, giving the impression that it's standard or acceptable.

This gradually reinforces prejudiced attitudes in viewers, making them more likely to tolerate or even engage in such behavior in real life. Take, for instance, the lengthy and convoluted history behind how various racial and ethnic groups have been portrayed in the media, most notably in Hollywood. Between 1960 and 1980, African Americans were commonly cast in roles that played up unfavorable stereotypes, such as drug dealers, pimps, or violent criminals. This practice continued well into the 1980s. These depictions frequently lacked nuance and subtlety, perpetuating damaging societal stereotypes about African Americans.

The effects of portrayals like this, based on stereotypes, can be long-lasting. They can mold the attitudes and biases of society, which can have real-world repercussions for the communities being represented. These poor images of African Americans in the media have helped contribute to the institutional racism that exists today, which affects everything from employment chances to encounters with the criminal justice system. However, the 1990s witnessed a trend toward images of African Americans in Hollywood that were more diverse and positive than in previous decades. Popular television programs such as "The Fresh Prince of Bel-Air," "Family Matters," and "The Cosby Show" portrayed African American households in a more positive and approachable manner.

In the film industry, actors like Denzel Washington, Morgan Freeman, and Halle Berry began to move away from traditional representations of their characters by taking on prominent roles in big movies. Despite these advancements, Hollywood still has a long way to go before portraying realistic, balanced, and diverse racial and cultural groups. There is a need for more narratives that accurately represent the enormous variety of identities and experiences that exist within these communities. These kinds of shifts in media representation have the potential to play a significant part in breaking stereotypes, lowering levels of bias, and fostering a more accepting society.

Numerous movies and TV shows feature characters who display ethnocentrism and prejudice, often glamorizing these values and influencing the behavior and attitudes of viewers. **Some notable examples include:**

Apu, who appears in "The Simpsons" (1989-present): has been controversial for a long time. Some people believe that the character perpetuates prejudices about South Asians. The announcement was made in 2020 that the show would no longer use white performers to provide the voices of non-white characters.

Netflix series "Iron Fist" (2017–2018): was criticized for depicting the white character Danny Rand as a skilled martial artist in a narrative heavily rooted in Asian culture. To avoid falling into the "white savior" stereotype, many reviewers believed that an actor of Asian heritage should have played the part.

Breaking Bad (2008–2013): this popular series was criticized for portraying many Hispanic characters as drug dealers or gang members, which might lead to damaging stereotypes if they are perpetuated. "Breaking Bad" ran for five seasons.

The United States vs. Billie Holiday (2021): received positive reviews for acting. Still, it was criticized for emphasizing Holiday's struggles with substance misuse more than her role as an important civil rights figure.

Because of how they are designed, social media platforms like Facebook and Twitter can amplify ethnocentrism and prejudice. These social media sites frequently place a higher priority on content that can drive engagement. It is possible for controversial or extreme views, particularly ethnocentric and discriminatory beliefs, to receive a lot of attention and engagement, leading these platforms to magnify the voices and opinions of those who hold these controversial or extreme views.

On these platforms, trolls can spread hate speech and target people based on religion, ethnicity, or other traits. Such content exposure and widespread dissemination might create an intolerant and discriminatory atmosphere. Because humans are responsible for developing algorithms, it is possible for these programs to unintentionally reflect and perpetuate the biases of the people who created them. If an algorithm prioritizes certain forms of human-generated material above others, this may contribute to the propagation of prejudice and ethnocentrism.

Recognizing prejudice within oneself can be challenging because these biases often operate unconsciously. However, self-awareness is the first step to change. **Here are some ways to identify if you might be harboring prejudice:**

Examine Your Comfort Zone: Do you feel uncomfortable or anxious around people different from you? Do you generally prefer to be around people who share your racial, ethnic, or cultural background? These could be signs of prejudice.

Observe Your Conversations: Do you often generalize about certain groups of people? Do you use derogatory language or jokes about other cultures or races, even if you think they're harmless? These behaviors indicate prejudice.

Check Your Social Circles: Are your friends and acquaintances mostly from your racial, ethnic, or social group? A lack of diversity in your social circle might indicate prejudice.

Notice Your Resistance: Do you feel defensive when someone challenges your views about a particular group of people? It could indicate prejudice if you find it hard to accept that you might be wrong or biased.

Examine Your Media Consumption: What types of people are represented in your media? Does it reinforce stereotypes or biases? Your media consumption can also reflect your prejudices.

If you identify signs of prejudice within yourself, you must not react with defensiveness or denial. Instead, use this as an opportunity for growth and learning.

Nevertheless, there is more to this journey than just recognizing these limiting worldviews. As we continue forward, we are going to explore vital techniques to change these viewpoints to cultivate a growth mindset, which has the potential to influence every aspect of your life positively. This book will guide you to a more prosperous and lively life, liberated from the shackles of restrictive worldviews. Let's set sail for a better illuminated and empowering horizon! Are you giddy about it? Most definitely, we are! Let's get started!

Chapter 7

The Power of Reflection: A Mirror to the Self

As we travel through life, we frequently rush from one moment to the next, never pausing to reflect on where we have been, where we are, or where we are going. Instead, we are constantly moving forward without thinking about these things. It's easy for us to get lost, like navigating without a compass. This is where introspection, or the mirror we often think of as a metaphor, comes into play.

Picture yourself standing in front of a mirror. When you look at your reflection, it reveals your image with unflinching honesty, bringing to light what is seen and what is not, and what is acknowledged and denied. The mirror has no preconceptions or preferences; it merely reflects reality, illuminating truths you already know and those you have concealed for your convenience. Much like this mirror, self-reflection is an illuminating tool for our minds, allowing us to scrutinize and comprehend our thoughts, actions, and beliefs unflinchingly and honestly. Self-reflection works similarly to this mirror.

In today's world, we are constantly being barraged with noise from the outside world, such as social media feeds filled with carefully curated lives, news outlets that spew polarizing narratives, societal pressures to conform to certain norms, and deeply ingrained cultural worldviews. This persistent barrage can easily obscure our internal voices, cloud our judgment, and reshape our perceptions of ourselves and the world around us.

In this complex landscape, self-reflection becomes a sanctuary, a sacred space where we can mute the outside world and tune into our inner selves. When we reflect, we grant ourselves permission to explore our mental landscapes, navigate our emotional seas, and scrutinize our embedded beliefs. We are no longer adrift in the sea of external influences; we become the captains of our journey.

Through self-reflection, we see ourselves not only as the world wants us to be but as individuals with unique worldviews and personal narratives. It allows us to untangle ourselves from the webs of societal expectations and cultural conditioning. It empowers us to differentiate between the worldviews imposed upon us and those we choose for ourselves.

Therefore, self-reflection is more than just the act of looking inward. It's a declaration of independence from the accepted norms of the world and a step toward self-actualization and liberation. By looking inward, we can see the invisible hand at work, the hidden goals, and the carefully orchestrated distractions, and then we can choose to ignore them and go in a different direction.

A rebellion against conformity and distraction in today's chaotic world is the act of self-reflection. It's necessary for liberation, combating harmful worldviews, and tearing down artificial barriers between people. Most importantly, it's how we expose and fight back against the world's larger agendas. It's the reflection we see when we strip away all the harmful influences and preconceived notions we've picked up.

Self-reflection is the mirror that shows us the role we've been playing and sheds light on the role we'd like to play. Reflection allows us to take stock of our lives, question the assumptions made about us, and rewrite our stories to reflect better who we are.

Arthur's Story:

Meet Arthur, a well-known bank's respected Chief Financial Officer (CFO). His sharp financial sense, analytical abilities, and knack for strategic planning had propelled him to the pinnacle of his profession. On the other hand, a glimpse into his personal life revealed a stark contrast, an image that did not bask in the glow of professional success. Arthur was firmly entrenched in a cynical and skeptical worldview. This perspective fueled his professional life, giving him the tools he needed to navigate the complex world of finance, questioning every figure and dissecting every statement. It had led him to make sound financial decisions, spotting risks long before others did.

This worldview, however, had seeped into his personal life, painting it with shades of doubt and distrust. Friendships were rare in Arthur's life, and those he did have were kept at arm's length, with friendships frequently marked by detachment and indifference. His skeptical outlook harmed his relationship with his daughter as well. He found it difficult to relate to her hopes and dreams, creating an emotional chasm that grew more comprehensive daily. Arthur came across a striking mirror in an antique store one day. Because of its exquisite craftsmanship, he brought it home and put it in his private study. Arthur was drawn to the mirror one quiet evening amidst the rustle of financial reports. The reflection he saw was more than just a copy of his physical self. It reflected his life, attitudes, and, most importantly, his worldview. The man staring back at him was a successful CFO of a major bank, cloaked in skepticism and cynicism.

The mirror reflected the strains in his friendships and the growing conflicts between him and his daughter, resulting from his skepticism. He saw himself in the mirror as the lone figure he had become, entrenched in cynicism, inadvertently pushing away those who wished to connect with him. His skepticism was no longer just a professional tool; it had turned into a personal barrier. Arthur's encounter with the mirror served as a harsh wake-up call. While skepticism and cynicism were valuable assets in his professional field, he realized that applying them indiscriminately to his personal life did more harm than good. He was unsure how to bridge the growing emotional gap because he was entrenched in his cynical worldview.

Arthur's story exemplifies how our worldviews have a profound and far-reaching impact on our professional and personal lives. It serves as a reminder to keep a healthy separation between our professional and personal lives. It emphasizes the power of introspection, as personified by the mirror, in revealing the actual state of our lives, regardless of how unpleasant that reality may be. We often find the first step toward understanding, change, and, ultimately, a balance between our professional and personal identities through honest self-observation.

Dee's Story:

In his relentless pursuit of wealth, Dee fell prey to dangerous habits. The bright lights of casinos, the adrenaline rush of dog racing tracks, and the lure of winning big with lottery tickets became his downfall. These addictions were initially just another avenue for Dee to fulfill his dreams of striking it rich, yet they quickly spiraled into a destructive obsession. His free time, which was already scarce due to his work commitments, was now entirely consumed by these vices. The thrill of gambling gave him a temporary high, a fleeting feeling of being on top of the world. But as soon as the moment passed, he was left with a more profound emptiness. His addiction drained his financial resources and created an emotional void. His desire to become rich through a shortcut fueled his addiction.

He poured more and more money into gambling, convinced that the next bet, the next ticket, would be his ticket to the wealthy life he aspired for. However, his dreams remained elusive while his debts continued to grow. Sitting alone in his cold, empty apartment one winter evening, he reflected on his life. Wrapped in a blanket, he looked at his reflection in the small, cracked mirror on the wall. The reflection stared back at him—a man consumed by his addictions, driven by a harmful worldview, who had lost everything in pursuing material wealth. A single tear rolled down his cheek as he came to terms with the state of his life. His wealth was gone, his friends had abandoned him, his wife had left, and his daughter was a stranger to him.

The casinos that were once his escape were now his prison, and the thrill of gambling had been replaced with a deep sense of regret and loss. Dee's story is a testament to the destructive power of harmful worldviews and addictions. It's a reminder that pursuing wealth, combined with addiction and unchecked materialism, can lead to devastating consequences. Dee's reflection in the mirror that cold winter night wasn't just a broken man; it was the personification of a fractured dream fueled by a harmful worldview. It's a mirror reflecting his past and present, offering a stark warning for the future.

These stories serve as a complex reality, reflecting the experiences of countless people worldwide. They are not alone in their difficulties; the consequences of these worldviews are felt globally. However, we can begin to effect change only by recognizing these effects, as Arthur and Dee did with the metaphorical mirror. Let us start our self-examination journey with the concept of the "Mirror."

The Metaphor of the Mirror:

Picture yourself standing in front of a mirror. It reflects your image and exposes all the truths, both the ones you are aware of and those you have been oblivious to up until now. Reflecting on one's thoughts, deeds, and beliefs serves as the mind's equivalent of a mirror and enables us to examine these aspects of ourselves. Taking the time to reflect allows us to focus inward in a world full of distractions and influences from the outside world. It enables us to see ourselves more accurately, not following how the world sees us, but as unique individuals whose points of view and worldviews are all their own.

The Significance of Self-Reflection:

Self-reflection is the process of introspection, examining our thoughts, feelings, and motivations. When we reflect, we dissect our experiences, ideas, and emotions. We question why we think the way we do, why we feel certain emotions, and why we've made specific choices. Self-reflection helps us identify our strengths and weaknesses, uncovering areas that may require change. This process is crucial in challenging and changing harmful worldviews we may unconsciously hold on to.

Recognizing Worldviews and Biases:

Drawing from the discussions in our previous chapters on recognizing worldviews and biases, we understand that each of us carries a unique perspective shaped by our inherent biases. These biases, silently influenced by our upbringing, societal norms, cultural context, and personal experiences, act as filters through which we interpret the world, forming our worldviews.

Self-Awareness: The Ultimate Goal:

The ultimate goal of self-reflection is to cultivate self-awareness. This is the state of being fully aware of your thoughts, feelings, and actions, and understanding why you think, feel, and act the way you do. With self-awareness, we gain a deeper understanding of ourselves, allowing for personal growth and change. Self-reflection is a powerful tool in our journey of challenging harmful worldviews. Like a mirror, it reflects our innermost thoughts and beliefs, allowing us to see ourselves. With this clarity, we can understand the impact of our worldviews, challenge them, and start making meaningful changes.

Stepping onto the trail of self-discovery, we are presented with a potent instrument for personal growth and self-awareness – Self-Examination. This inward journey might feel daunting, yet it's the key to unlocking the door to understanding our authentic selves. Embarking on this exploration can help us uncover our biases, challenge our worldviews, and ultimately shape our evolution.

However, venturing into the depths of self-discovery requires a guide, a structure that can steer us through the murky waters of introspection. These steps are not a rigid framework but a flexible map to navigate this personal voyage. So, pull up the anchor of doubt, hoist the sails of courage, and let us set sail on this enlightening journey of self-examination with these carefully designed steps.

1. Find a Quiet Space:

Before you begin the process of self-examination, find a quiet space where you can sit undisturbed. This will help you focus your mind and promote a sense of calm.

2. Start with a Mindfulness Practice:

Begin your self-examination process by grounding yourself in the present moment. You should practice a few minutes of mindfulness meditation, focusing on your breath or bodily sensations. This practice can help clear your mind and prepare you for self-reflection.

3. Ask Open-Ended Questions:

The key to self-examination lies in asking the right questions. Ask open-ended questions about your beliefs, values, actions, and emotions.

For example, you might ask:
- What values are most important to me?
- How do these values influence my actions?
- What belief systems do I hold?

How have these beliefs shaped my worldview?
What are the emotions I experience most frequently?
How do these emotions affect my interactions with others?

4. Reflect on Your Past:

Your past can offer valuable insights into your present self. Reflect on significant past events or experiences and how they have shaped your beliefs, values, and behaviors.

5. Use a Journal:

Journaling can be an excellent tool for self-examination. Writing your thoughts down can help clarify your feelings and ideas, and re-reading your entries over time can provide insights into your growth and change.

6. Seek Feedback:

While self-examination is a personal journey, seeking feedback from someone you are close to, such as a significant other, family member, or friend, can provide an outside perspective that might illuminate blind spots in your self-understanding.

7. Challenge Your Own Beliefs:

As you identify your beliefs and values, challenge them. Are there other perspectives you might not have considered? Are there beliefs you hold that might be harmful or limiting?

8. Plan for Change:

Finally, use your self-examination as a basis for personal growth. If you've identified beliefs or behaviors that you want to change, plan how to do so. This might involve setting specific goals, seeking support, or engaging in further self-education.

Remember, self-examination is a journey rather than a destination. Be patient with yourself and remember to celebrate your progress.

Now that we understand the 5 top impacting worldviews and have conducted an open, honest self-evaluation, let's discuss one of the three pillars to a free and satisfying life by removing these unseen shackles by these world revies. The first pillar is the foundation.

Having journeyed through the labyrinth of the five most influential worldviews and casting an unflinching, introspective glance upon ourselves, we now find ourselves at a significant juncture. It's time to enter the illuminating world of the three pillars forming the bedrock of a fulfilling and free life. These pillars act as our beacon, guiding us out of the murky shadows cast by these worldviews, helping us shatter the unseen shackles restraining our spirits. As we stand on the threshold of this transformative chapter, we encounter the first of these powerful pillars.

In the next chapter, we dive into the intricacies of the LIGHT Pathway, a transformative journey that will guide you toward wholeness and freedom. Each step along this pathway is designed to shed light on the areas impacted by limiting worldviews and empower you to embrace a balanced, fulfilled life anchored in God's Word and enriched by meaningful relationships.

In the subsequent chapters, we will delve into each step of the LIGHT Pathway. We will provide practical tools, biblical insights, and real-life stories illuminating your path and empowering you to break free from limiting worldviews. Get ready to embrace the LIGHT and embark on a life-changing journey toward wholeness and freedom!

I refer to this initial pillar as the 'Foundation.' It is more than a mere structural underpinning; it's a solid bedrock grounded in leadership principles and God's words. It's the basis upon which we can dismantle harmful worldviews, replacing them with a more constructive, liberating perspective. So, let us delve deeper into this 'Foundation,' exploring its potential to usher in a profound shift in our lives.

Chapter 8

The LIGHT Pathway (Luminary Foundation, Inclusive Bonds, Generous Empathy, Harmonious Evolution, and Transformative Growth)

As you progress through the five phases of the LIGHT Pathway, you will start on an incredible journey toward wholeness, freedom, and spiritual development. Taking another step along this path illuminates another aspect of your existence, unveiling previously buried characteristics, sentiments, and potential that you were unaware you possessed. It is a journey that promises not just to change you but also to transform you, to lift you from where you are now to where you have the potential to be.

The LIGHT Pathway is neither a quick fix nor a direct path to enlightenment; it is a lifetime commitment to one's continual personal and spiritual development. Unchaining yourself from the hidden chains of the world is an awakening. It is about reflecting the divine light of wisdom, love, and truth on your chosen life path. It is about forging bonds of oneness, nurturing empathy, inviting change, commemorating growth, persevering in adversity, and striving for divine union.

The Luminary Foundation, also known as Ground Zero, is where we begin our inquiry into the LIGHT Pathway.

Your spiritual path began at Ground Zero, a place where new beginnings and an infinite number of opportunities can be found. It is the foundation upon which we build the remainder of our lives, the platform upon which we establish the cornerstone of our spiritual building. We commune with the divine light of the Word of God at this place, enabling its knowledge, love, and truth to serve as a compass for us as we travel.

This chapter is dedicated to helping you understand the significance of Ground Zero in your personal and professional lives. It is about becoming acquainted with spiritual truths and concepts that will serve as a compass for you, guiding you through the various stages and transitions you encounter. We'll look at how these principles influence your decisions, how you connect with people, and how you see the world.

The question now is, are you ready to go on this magnificent journey? Are you willing to allow the holy light of God's Word to shine into and guide your life? If you answered yes, take a step forward into Ground Zero, and the journey along the LIGHT Pathway can now officially begin.

Phase 1 - Luminary Foundation - Ground Zero (God's Word)

Someone once said that life is like constructing a building from the ground up. The construction of life, just like the construction of any other building, begins with a foundation. This foundation needs to be unyielding to bear the weight of our aspirations, experiences, and difficulties when they are added to it. As we travel through life, we come into contact with various worldviews, some inspiring and motivating us, while others stifle our growth, obstruct our advancement, and obscure our perspectives. To successfully navigate these, we need a solid foundation unmoved by the shifting sands of societal norms and the personal complexities that life throws at us. A basis based on truth, wisdom, and universally applicable principles. This sort of basis is made available to us through the reading of God's Word.

This isn't just a foundational stage—an awakening, an enlightening. Ground Zero isn't about physical location or a stagnant state of being; rather, it's a vibrant, radiant beacon forming your journey's basis. Here, we use God's Word as a divine hammer, breaking the chains of the five limiting worldviews we explored earlier in this journey.

The chains of the Fixed Mindset, Fear-Driven Mentality, Hollow Pursuit of Materialism and Consumerism, Downward Spiral of Pessimism and Negativity, and Barrier of Ethnocentrism and Prejudice all dissolve under the radiant light of divine wisdom.

God's Word, in its profound depth and breadth, offers us a fresh perspective. A perspective that sees potential, not limitations; that is driven by faith, not fear; that finds fulfillment in purpose and service, not material acquisition; that thrives on optimism and positivity, not pessimism and negativity; and that champions unity, understanding, and global harmony over prejudice and discrimination.

As you venture out, Ground Zero acts as your spiritual compass, the Divine Word etching values, and principles into your heart. Here, you don't merely read God's Word; you interact with it, question it, wrestle with it, and most importantly, integrate it into your worldviews.

The Luminary Foundation phase challenges you to examine your beliefs, biases, and prejudices under the illuminating light of God's Word. It encourages you to replace limiting beliefs with empowering divine truths, thus rewriting the narrative of your life. This stage prompts an exploration of spiritual truths beyond religious doctrines, prompting a transformation in perspective that is deeply freeing and liberating.

Ground Zero is the stage where the shift begins, where the chains of the five restrictive worldviews begin to weaken and eventually break. With the light of God's Word, you start on the path to freedom, on a journey towards a wholesome and fulfilling life, unshackled by limiting beliefs and worldviews.

The Word of God is a treasure trove of divine wisdom, a sanctuary of comfort, a moral compass, and an unerring guide amidst the uncertainties of life. It offers a lens to perceive our circumstances anew, a weapon to combat harmful worldviews, and a beacon that guides us toward growth, bravery, contentment, optimism, and empathy. The scriptures in the Bible address the worldviews we've discussed earlier and provide practical, applicable principles to counter them effectively.

Fixed Mindset:

One of the great examples of God's word serving as a foundation can be found in **Psalm 119:105**: "Your word is a lamp to my feet and a light to my path." Picture a woman lost in the vast expanse of a dense forest, the Fixed Mindset her compass, guiding her deeper into confusion and stagnation. But when she stumbles upon this verse, a lamp is lit, guiding her out of the imprisoning forest and onto the path of growth and limitless potential. The parable of the talents (**Matthew 25:14-30**) illustrates the dangers of a fixed mindset. Imagine a young man named Samuel who had a deep passion for music. However, due to past failures and criticism, he developed a fixed mindset, believing he was not talented enough to pursue a music career. One day, his friend Nathan encouraged him to audition for a local talent show. Samuel hesitated, but with a newfound determination, he embraced a growth mindset. He practiced relentlessly, honed his skills, and eventually won the competition, gaining recognition for his incredible musical talent. Through this experience, Samuel learned that his potential was not fixed but rather could be expanded through effort and perseverance.

Philippians 4:13: "I can do all things through Christ who strengthens me." This verse became Samuel's mantra, reminding him that with God's strength, he could overcome any self-imposed limitations and embrace a growth mindset.

Meet Ethan, a young aspiring writer who believed he lacked the talent to pursue his dreams. Despite receiving positive feedback on his stories, he doubted his abilities and kept his writing hidden. One day, he stumbled upon the story of Clara, a bestselling author who faced rejection numerous times before achieving success. Inspired by Clara's journey, Ethan decided to challenge his fixed mindset. He began to meditate on the scripture verse **Romans 12:6a**, which reminded him that God had given each person unique gifts and talents. With this newfound perspective, Ethan stepped out in faith, sharing his writing with others and embracing constructive feedback. His writing flourished as he leaned on God's strength, leading to publishing opportunities and a newfound belief in his abilities.

Romans 12:6a: "We have different gifts, according to the grace given to each of us."

Fear-Driven Mentality:

Let's meet Emma, a young woman struggling with a fear-driven mentality. She dreamed of starting her own business but was paralyzed by the fear of failure and uncertainty. One day, she came across the story of Peter walking on water (**Matthew 14:22-33**). Inspired by Peter's boldness, she took a leap of faith and launched her business venture. Though faced with challenges and moments of doubt, Emma relied on her faith and God's guidance to overcome her fears. With time, her business flourished, and Emma discovered the immense joy and fulfillment that came from stepping out of the boat and into the unknown.

2 Timothy 1:7 - "For God gave us a spirit not of fear but of power and love and self-control." This verse became Emma's source of strength, reminding her that fear should not dictate her decisions, but rather, she should embrace the power and love of God to conquer her fears.

Let's meet Olivia, a dedicated nurse who longed to volunteer overseas but was held back by fear of the unknown. Intrigued by the story of Gabriel, a nurse who overcame similar fears and made a difference in impoverished communities, Olivia sought guidance from God's Word. She found solace in **Isaiah 41:10**, which reminded her that God is with her and would strengthen and help her. Encouraged by this promise, Olivia mustered the courage to embark on a medical mission. Her fear transformed into boldness as she relied on God's guidance and leaned on His promises. Olivia discovered her ability to adapt, connect with others, and provide essential healthcare in underserved areas, profoundly impacting the lives of those she served.

Isaiah 41:10 - "So do not fear, for I am with you; do not be dismayed, for I am your God. I will strengthen and help you and uphold you with my righteous right hand."

Hollow Pursuit of Materialism and Consumerism:

Meet Daniel, a successful corporate executive who seemed to have a luxurious lifestyle, a sprawling mansion, and all the trappings of material wealth. However, he felt empty and fulfilled. One day, Daniel stumbled upon the parable of the rich fool (**Luke 12:13-21**). This story resonated deeply with him as he realized that pursuing material possessions was meaningless. Inspired to make a change, Daniel redirected his focus towards more meaningful pursuits, such as philanthropy and helping others in need. Through his acts of generosity, Daniel found a sense of purpose and fulfillment that far exceeded the shallow allure of materialism

Matthew 6:19-21 - "Do not store up for yourselves treasures on earth...but store up for yourselves treasures in heaven...For where your treasure is, there your heart will also be." These verses became Daniel's guiding principles, reminding him to invest in eternal treasures that transcend material wealth.

Enter the life of Marcus, a successful businessman who amassed wealth and possessions but felt an emptiness deep within. One day, he came across the story of Olivia, a philanthropist who used her resources to uplift marginalized communities. Inspired by Olivia's selflessness, Marcus turned to **1 Timothy 6:17-19** for guidance. The scripture reminded him that true fulfillment comes from being generous and sharing what he had with others. Marcus decided to shift his focus from material accumulation to making a lasting impact. He established a foundation that supported education initiatives, healthcare programs, and sustainable development projects. As he followed God's call to be a good steward of his resources, Marcus also discovered a sense of purpose and fulfillment that transcended material wealth.

1 Timothy 6:17-19 - "Command those who are rich in this present world not to be arrogant nor to put their hope in wealth, which is so uncertain, but to put their hope in God, who richly provides us with everything for our enjoyment. Command them to do good, to be rich in good deeds, and to be generous and willing to share. In this way, they will lay up treasure for themselves as a firm foundation for the coming age so that they may take hold of the life that is truly life."

Downward Spiral of Pessimism and Negativity:

Now let's meet Sarah, a talented artist struggling with a perpetual sense of pessimism and negativity. Every setback or criticism sent her spiraling into self-doubt and despair. One day, she came across the account of the twelve spies sent to explore Canaan (**Numbers 13 & 14**). Inspired by the courageous faith of Joshua and Caleb, she decided to confront her negative mindset and embrace a more positive outlook.

Sarah started a gratitude journal, focusing on the blessings and beauty around her. Over time, she discovered that shifting her perspective and dwelling on positive thoughts led to a renewed sense of hope, creativity, and a newfound resilience in the face of challenges. As Sarah embraced a more optimistic mindset, her artwork began to flourish. She found inspiration in even the smallest details and used her talent to uplift others through her vibrant and joyful creations.

Philippians 4:8 - "Finally, brothers and sisters, whatever is true, whatever is noble, whatever is right, whatever is pure, whatever is lovely, whatever is admirable—if anything is excellent or praiseworthy—think about such things." This scripture became Sarah's daily reminder to focus her thoughts on the positive and uplifting aspects of life, allowing her to break free from the downward spiral of pessimism.

How about Sophia, a talented musician who faced rejection and setbacks throughout her career? Overwhelmed by negativity, she questioned her abilities and contemplated giving up on her passion. In a moment of despair, Sophia stumbled upon the story of Daniel, a renowned composer who persevered through adversity and became a musical icon.

Inspired by Daniel's resilience, Sophia turned to **Philippians 4:13**, which reminded her that she could do all things through Christ who strengthens her. With renewed faith and confidence, Sophia committed to focusing on her strengths and surrounding herself with positive influences. As she leaned on God's promises, Sophia transformed her setbacks into stepping stones, ultimately achieving recognition and inspiring others with her uplifting melodies.

Philippians 4:13 - "I can do all this through him who gives me strength."

Barrier of Ethnocentrism and Prejudice:

Let's journey with Michael, a young man whose life was deeply influenced by the barrier of ethnocentrism and prejudice. Growing up in a community with limited exposure to different cultures, he held biases and misconceptions about people from diverse backgrounds. One day, he encountered the parable of the Good Samaritan (**Luke 10:25-37**). Struck by the compassion and love shown by the Samaritan towards a stranger in need, Michael began to question his prejudices.

Inspired to bridge the gap between cultures, he actively sought out opportunities to connect with individuals from different ethnicities and backgrounds. Through these encounters, Michael developed deep friendships and gained a broader perspective on the richness of human diversity. His changed worldview allowed him to appreciate the unique contributions and experiences of people from all walks of life.

Acts 10:34-35 - "Then Peter began to speak: 'I now realize how true it is that God does not show favoritism but accepts from every nation the one who fears him and does what is right.'" This scripture became Michael's guiding light, reminding him that God values everyone regardless of ethnicity and challenging him to break down the barrier of ethnocentrism in his own heart.

Journey with Maya, a young woman who grew up in a community marked by cultural divisions and biases. Intrigued by the story of Amir, a social activist who dedicated his life to promoting understanding and unity, Maya sought wisdom from God's Word. She discovered **Galatians 3:28**, which emphasized that there is no distinction between people of different backgrounds in Christ. Armed with this truth, Maya embarked on a journey of compassion and empathy.

She actively sought opportunities to engage with people from diverse backgrounds, volunteered in community outreach programs, and initiated dialogues to bridge divides. Through these experiences, Maya became a catalyst for positive change, embracing the beauty of different cultures, fostering meaningful connections, and breaking down the barrier of ethnocentrism.

Galatians 3:28 - "There is neither Jew nor Gentile, neither slave nor free, nor is there male and female, for you are all one in Christ Jesus."

These stories demonstrate how the transformative power of God's Word and personal experiences can break the chains of limiting worldviews. Through scriptures and parables, individuals gain insight, inspiration, and guidance to overcome the five worldviews, embrace a more expansive perspective, and live a life grounded in love, purpose, and unity.

Building this foundation does not imply that life will be without its challenges. Trials and tribulations are an intrinsic part of the human experience. However, a life anchored on the rock of God's word equips you to weather these storms with grace, resilience, and unwavering faith. So, as we continue this journey, let's hold steadfastly to this foundation, harnessing the power of God's Word as we press forward toward the freedom and fulfillment, we all aspire to attain.

Applying God's armor is a part of the foundation that is a powerful way to break the chains of worldviews and stand firm in your faith. Here's a guide on how to apply each piece of God's armor, as described in **Ephesians 6:10-18**.

The Belt of Truth: Embrace the truth of God's Word and align your beliefs and values with it. Study the Scriptures diligently and seek to understand the principles and teachings of the Bible. Reject the deceptive lies of worldly worldviews by anchoring yourself in the truth of God's Word.

The Breastplate of Righteousness: Live a life of righteousness, seeking to align your actions and attitudes with God's standards. Reject the sinful desires and temptations that the world presents. Allow the righteousness of Christ to cover and protect your heart, guarding it against the world's influences.

The Gospel of Peace Shoes: Walk in peace and spread the message of the Gospel wherever you go. Seek peace, reconciliation, and love in your interactions with others. Remain steadfast in your faith and share the hope of salvation through Jesus Christ with those around you.

The Helmet of Salvation: Guard your mind with the assurance of salvation through Jesus Christ. Let the truth of your identity in Christ shield your thoughts from the lies and distortions of worldly worldviews. Fix your mind on the eternal hope and salvation found in Christ, protecting yourself from discouragement and despair.

The Sword of the Spirit: The sword represents the Word of God. Study and meditate on Scripture, allowing it to dwell richly in your heart. Use the truth of God's Word to counteract the lies and deceptions of worldly worldviews. Apply the Scriptures in prayer, in times of temptation, and when you need guidance and wisdom.

Now that your wear God's armor, here are some practical additional steps and insights on how to apply and grow your relationship with God's Word to combat the worldviews and live a full and satisfying life.

Daily Devotional Time: Set aside dedicated time each day for personal devotions. Create a quiet and comfortable space oo read, reflect, pray, and meditate on God's Word. Make it a habit to seek God's presence and wisdom through intentional engagement with Scripture.

Study and Reflection: Engage in deeper study of the Bible by utilizing study resources such as commentaries, concordances, and study guides. Reflect on the meaning and application of the passages you read. Ask questions, seek understanding, and allow the Holy Spirit to illuminate the truths revealed in God's Word.

Journaling: Keep a journal to record your thoughts, insights, and prayers as you interact with Scripture. Write down key verses that resonate with you, personal reflections, and prayers of gratitude or petitions. Journaling helps to deepen your understanding and creates a tangible record of your spiritual growth journey.

Memorization: Select meaningful verses or passages and commit them to memory. Memorizing Scripture allows God's Word to dwell richly within you and equips you with a reservoir of truth to combat worldly perspectives. Write down verses on notecards or use a Bible memory app to assist in the memorization process.

Application and Action: The true power of God's Word is in its application to our lives. As you read and study Scripture, identify practical ways to apply its teachings daily. Seek opportunities to live out God's love, forgiveness, compassion, and justice principles. Let your actions align with the values and truths in the Word of God.

Accountability and Community: Surround yourself with fellow believers seeking to grow in their relationship with God. Join a small group, Bible study, or accountability group where you can discuss Scripture, share insights, and support one another. Community engagement fosters encouragement, accountability, and a deeper understanding of God's Word.

Prayer: Prayer is vital in growing your relationship with God's Word. Before you begin reading, pray for the Holy Spirit to guide your understanding and illuminate the truths of Scripture. Invite the Holy Spirit to reveal any areas of your life where worldly worldviews have taken hold and ask for His help to combat them.

Consistency and Persistence: Growing your relationship with God's Word is a lifelong journey. It requires consistency and persistence. Set realistic goals for reading and studying the Bible and commit to them. Even when you don't feel particularly motivated, prioritize your time with God and trust that He will honor your commitment.

Here are a few examples of reading plans to help you start your connection with God:

New Testament in 30 Days:

- Day 1-5: Read the Gospel of Matthew
- Day 6-10: Read the Gospel of Mark
- Day 11-15: Read the Gospel of Luke
- Day 16-20: Read the Gospel of John
- Day 21-24: Read the Acts of the Apostles
- Day 25-28: Read selected Epistles (e.g., Romans, Corinthians, Galatians, Ephesians)
- Day 29-30: Read the Book of Revelation
- Psalms and Proverbs in 30 Days:
- Day 1-15: Read five Psalms each day (e.g., Day 1 - Psalms 1-5, Day 2 - Psalms 6-10, and so on)
- Day 16-30: Read one chapter of Proverbs each day (e.g., Day 16 - Proverbs 1, Day 17 - Proverbs 2, and so on)

Chronological Bible Reading Plan:
Day 1-30: Begin reading from Genesis and follow the chronological order of events as presented in the Bible.

Topical Bible Study Plan:
Choose a specific topic of interest, such as love, forgiveness, faith, or wisdom. Search for relevant verses and passages related to the chosen topic. Read and meditate on a few verses or passages daily, reflecting on their meaning and how they apply to your life.

Gospels Reading Plan:
Read through the four Gospels (Matthew, Mark, Luke, and John) in order, spending a set amount of time each day (e.g., 15 minutes) until you complete each Gospel.

The most important aspect is approaching your reading with an open heart, seeking to connect with God, and allowing His Word to transform your life.

Remember, developing a deep and meaningful relationship with God's Word is a personal and unique journey. Allow the Scriptures to shape your thoughts, transform your perspectives, and empower you to live a life that is grounded in God's truth and free from the limitations of worldly worldviews.

Congratulations! You've taken your first steps on the LIGHT Pathway, illuminating your journey with the divine light of the Luminary Foundation, Ground Zero. You've begun to anchor your life in spiritual truths and principles, and now it's time to take the next step. As we move forward, we venture into a just as crucial to our wholeness and freedom - the Realm of Relationships.

Chapter 9

Inclusive Bonds: The Web (Building and Maintaining Relationships)

"Inclusive Bonds: The Web" is a stage that invites you to go beyond yourself and explore the rich strands of interactions that connect us to the world around us. At this point, you will realize that you are not an island but a node in an extensive, interconnected network, a vital component of the Web of Life.

The Internet is a fantastic metaphor for our relationships with our families, friends, coworkers, and, most importantly, God. Each thread represents a relationship, a bond, with its distinct power, vitality, and resonance. These threads weave together to build a web that offers support, promotes growth, and contributes to a healthy and satisfied life.

You will learn how to build and nurture these relationships during this period. You will learn the art of relationship building and how to form supportive, meaningful partnerships. You'll discover the intricacies of emotional intelligence, the skill of effective communication, and the importance of empathy in forming powerful friendships.

However, not all of the threads on our Web are strong. Some relationships may be strained or dissolved due to numerous life situations or misunderstandings. This stage also emphasizes the significance of mending and restoring these frayed relationships. You'll discover how to repair damaged relationships, let go of old hurts, and rebuild trust. This will enhance the Web that connects you to others, bolstering your journey toward completeness and freedom.

Each relationship, bond, and interaction on the Internet provides growth and learning opportunities. It's a complex dance of giving and receiving, comprehending and being comprehended, and loving and being loved. The Inclusive Bonds stage is an essential phase on the LIGHT Pathway that helps you understand that your connections are more than just a part of your life; they are threads that weave the fabric of your existence.

Throughout my 25-year career in information technology and retail leadership roles, I have had the pleasure of meeting many people. These were people from many walks of life, representing various ethnic backgrounds, genders, ages, and backgrounds. With its many colors and tones, this kaleidoscope of humankind improved my life in more ways than I could have imagined.

As a leader, I led several small groups, helping them through Bible studies and leadership training. During these encounters, I discovered a common thread that connected us all: our shared human experiences and struggles, especially those related to our worldviews.

Worldviews function similarly to the glasses through which we interpret reality, shaping our perceptions, beliefs, and actions. Many variables influence them, from our childhood and culture to personal experiences and religious views. Despite our various backgrounds and life circumstances, we struggled with similar challenges connected to these worldviews in our small groups.

However, I only realized our perspective's enormous impact on our relationships afterward. Whether in professional or personal contacts, I noticed how opposing worldviews might strain links, causing misunderstandings and disputes. It became clear that healthy, lasting relationships were about more than compatibility or common interests.

It also required comprehending, appreciating, and navigating the complexity of other worldviews.

In the exciting game of life, time is the currency we use to achieve our objectives. Time is the fundamental component we actively invest in our activities, whether pursuing a potential romantic partner, developing our careers, or raising our firstborn. We recognize that to establish something significant, whether a relationship or a job, we must first commit time. It's a universal fact that applies to all facets of our lives.

Think about the start of a love relationship. The early days are characterized by an exuberant interchange of time and energy as two people compete for each other's devotion. They participate in activities they would not normally do, adjust to each other's preferences, and devote significant time to nurturing the developing relationship. The same logic applies to professional advancement. Building relationships with colleagues, supervisors, and subordinates, comprehending the complexities of the workplace, and striving for excellence all necessitate significant time investment.

The birth of a kid creates a special thrill that motivates us to devote our time to fostering this new bond. Friendships, like marriages, become stronger over time due to shared experiences, mutual support, and the joy of companionship.

However, when the initial "game" is won, a vital point of reflection develops. We've created the relationship, landed the job, raised the child, and formed the friendship - what now? This is where many of us need to correct things. The difficulty is not only in establishing these relationships but also in maintaining and growing them.

Too often, we revert to patterns determined by our worldviews, frequently formed by cultural conceptions such as materialism and consumerism. We find ourselves seeking money and power, often at the expense of our relationships. But does winning the game imply that we should no longer invest our time?

Our sense of what is significant changes as we age, and our priorities fluctuate. We tend to spend our time on what appears to be the most important, often disregarding other equally vital elements of our lives. I, on the other hand, believe in the concept of balance. Keeping ties with your children, parents, siblings, close friends, and even new friends should be as vital as saving your professional network.

Giving up on relationships when we believe we have won the game is not the answer. Instead, we should devote time and energy to consistently sustaining and cultivating these ties. It is about understanding that the game only finishes when we achieve our immediate objectives. Instead, it transforms into a more rewarding path in which the emphasis moves from winning to growing, from conquering to nurturing.

Relationships are at the heart of our being, shaping our experiences, perceptions, and development. They are not limited to one aspect of our lives but encompass multiple personal, professional, and spiritual dimensions. The significance of fostering these relationships becomes apparent when considering their impact on our well-being and personal progress.

Family, friends, love partners, and peers all play essential roles in our daily life. These connections provide us with emotional support, a sense of belonging, and chances for personal growth. They shape our character and worldview by teaching us empathy, respect, and kindness.

Professional relationships with colleagues, mentors, and networks provide career growth, learning, and collaboration opportunities. They promote teamwork, mutual respect, and shared goals, all of which contribute to a healthier and more productive workplace.

Relationships we form on our spiritual journey are equally vital. Our relationship with God, or the spiritual entity we believe in, gives us purpose, direction, and inner calm. It's a bond that frequently directs our actions, forms our values, and affects our vision of the world.

Our spiritual links also extend to our fellow humans. Many spiritual teachings emphasize the value of compassion, love, and service to others. They inspire us to cultivate connections based on kindness, empathy, and mutual respect, contributing to our spiritual progress.

Building and maintaining these relationships, like every other element of life, takes time, effort, and commitment. Understanding the other person, respecting their viewpoints, and developing the link via shared experiences and open conversation are all part of it.

It entails seeking a greater connection with the Divine, learning spiritual teachings, and embodying them in our interactions with others in our spiritual relationships. It is about fostering our spiritual development while also contributing to the well-being of others.

Relationships are critical in many aspects of life. They help us with our happiness, personal development, career achievement, and spiritual evolution. However, it is vital to recognize that the quality of these relationships is more essential than their quantity. A few meaningful, loving connections can be more gratifying and enriching than many shallow ones.

Relationships are a dynamic combination of building, maintaining, and evolving. They are not static entities but dynamic ecosystems that alter and grow over time. However, when social media plays such an important role in our modern age, the concept of relationships and how we see them has changed dramatically.

Social media platforms have evolved into new arenas for relationship development. They enable us to communicate with people worldwide, opening us to a world of prospective friendships, romantic partnerships, and professional networks. However, it's critical to recognize that the nature of these platforms, driven by likes, followers, and viral trends, can gradually change our worldviews and how we approach relationships.

The instant gratification social media sites offer might lead to a 'get what you want' mentality. We want immediate results - abundant likes on our posts, increased followers, and speedy responses to our messages. This perspective, reinforced by social media platform algorithms, might lead us to see relationships as transactional, as a means to an end. We put time and effort into creating these relationships because of what we can benefit from them rather than because of their fundamental value.

This mindset, however, overlooks a vital part of relationships: their maintenance and evolution over time. Relationships are not static; they are live, breathing things that must be nurtured and cared for. They need time, effort, and genuine connection, which cannot be measured by likes or following.

Furthermore, the social media worldview frequently stresses the chase of money, power, status, and material items, pushing us away from the fundamental nature of relationships - genuine connection, mutual respect, shared experiences, and emotional support.

The problem, therefore, becomes navigating our social media-shaped worldviews while creating and maintaining meaningful relationships. It's about understanding these platforms' limitations and ensuring they don't define how we approach relationships.

First, we must recognize that while social media can be an effective tool for interacting with others, it must maintain the depth and richness of face-to-face encounters. We must devote time and energy to cultivating offline relationships and building connections beyond the digital arena.

Second, we must abandon the 'get what you want' mentality and approach relationships with an eye toward mutual growth and support. We must invest in our relationships to 'win' and grow together, learn from one another, and support one another through life's ups and downs.

Finally, we must question the worldviews espoused by social media sites. Rather than being misled by trends or popular opinion, we must clarify our values and beliefs and ensure they guide our actions and decisions.

In the age of social media, building and maintaining relationships needs us to be mindful of our worldviews, to be willing to commit time and effort, and to respect the inherent worth of our relationships. It is about knowing that relationships are not a game to be won but rather a journey to be treasured, a path of mutual growth, support, and understanding.

Here are some examples of how social media influences relationships:

Constant Connection: Social media helps us to stay in touch with people no matter where they are. This can help us sustain long-distance connections and keep in touch with folks we may not see regularly. However, it can lead to an 'always on' mentality in which people feel compelled to continually check their social media, thus leading to stress, worry, and less face-to-face engagement.

Inadequacy and Comparison: Social media highlight reels can lead to comparisons and feelings of inadequacy. This can strain relationships because people may feel pressured to live up to a romantic image of life that does not correspond to reality.

Cyberbullying and Trolling: Unfortunately, social media can also serve as a platform for negative behaviors such as cyberbullying and trolling, which can have severe consequences for relationships and mental health.

Time Consumption: Excessive time spent on social media might detract from face-to-face interactions and lead to disregarding physical connections.

As a result, while social media has made it simpler to connect with others, utilizing it as a tool rather than a replacement for in-person encounters is critical. Traditional relationship maintenance and building techniques should be supplemented, not replaced, by social media. It necessitates using it with caution, respecting the boundaries of others, and knowing its possible impact on mental health.

Ben's Story:

My friend Ben, a contact from my networking circles, expressed his difficulty with me over a casual lunch one day. He had trouble connecting with his adolescent daughter, and the gap grew more significant by the day. As he detailed his predicament, I saw a man dealing with grief, a father seeking a connection that had escaped him.

Curiosity piqued, and I inquired about Ben's relationship with his daughter when she was younger. "I was always there for her initially," he said, bewildered. She was our first child." But as we dug deeper into his story, a new image emerged.

Ben said that things changed when his son arrived two years later. His son was into sports, which Ben also enjoyed. This shared interest pushed them closer together, and Ben began spending more time with his kid, strengthening their bond via similar interests. Unknowingly, he had started a winnable game with his kid in the hopes that he would become a great soccer player.

On the other hand, Ben felt that because his kid was a girl, she would automatically be closer to her mother. He was unaware of the hole he was leaving in his relationship with his daughter. He unintentionally sidelined her, leaving her feeling unappreciated and disconnected.

I asked Ben, "Do you see how you got into this situation?" I questioned Ben. You were preoccupied with your son, viewing him as a winnable game based on similar interests, and you expected your daughter would be okay with her mother. However, you have unwittingly created a divide between yourself and your daughter."

Ben remained silent, the gravity of the situation hitting in. His eyes revealed a rising comprehension of the accidental negligence that had led to his current circumstance.

Ben's story is a sad reminder of the careful balance required to sustain connections, particularly those inside families. Every person, every child, requires individualized attention and emotional sustenance. Preference for one relationship over another based on shared interests or ease of connection might have unforeseen repercussions. It is about realizing that relationships are not contests to be won but rather magnificent journeys of mutual growth and shared experiences.

While Ben's connection with his daughter may take some time to repair, the first step has been accomplished - recognition. It is never too late to restore broken relationships. Ben can bridge the gap with his daughter and reconnect on a deeper level with understanding, patience, and constant effort. His narrative demonstrates that every relationship is valuable and worthy of our time, effort, and compassion. Most significantly, it reminds us that love should never be a favoritism game but rather an inclusive relationship that embraces everybody.

Ben began to reveal more about his life as we completed our lunch. He described how his attention gradually turned to his son and his work. Other aspects of his life began to suffer as he strived to achieve his career and coach his son in soccer. He was attempting to juggle too many balls, and some inevitably fell. One of them was his bond with his daughter.

Ben's wife was a strong and independent woman who skillfully managed the home and their daughter. Ben thought his focus was best spent at work and with his kid, who needed instruction on the soccer field. Now, the home front appeared to be under control. He felt he was spending his time correctly, guaranteeing financial stability for his family and developing his son's athletic potential.

The more he spoke, though, the more precise the oversight became. His life was like a puzzle, with some pieces getting more attention than others. His relationship with his son and work were well-fitting puzzle pieces, while his relationship with his daughter, wife, and even his interests and friends were overlooked.

Ben's tale exemplifies how easily we can become engrossed in some aspects of our lives while unknowingly disregarding others. Humans are drawn to situations where we may see immediate benefits and tangible effects. Ben's work was thriving, and his son's soccer abilities increased. These became known as his 'winnable games.'

Relationships, especially with family, aren't founded on wins and losses. They thrive on shared experiences, mutual respect, and equality. They necessitate continual work and attention rather than being divided based on interests or conveniences. Ben had missed this in his pursuit of specific ambitions.

His daughter, growing up and needing her father's emotional care, felt neglected. The lack of attention made her feel less appreciated, which contributed to the estrangement Ben was now experiencing. His wife, who had taken over management of the home and their kid, was left wishing for a partner to share the joys and hardships of life. Due to his frequent unavailability, his buddies, with whom he had shared a strong bond, had become simply acquaintances.

It is challenging to navigate life while balancing work obligations, personal interests, and relationships. It's a delicate skill that takes deliberate work, time management, and a clear grasp of what is essential. Ben's epiphany came at a steep cost: he was estranged from his daughter.

But hope is never lost. With awareness comes the ability to change. Ben now has the opportunity to reassess his priorities and rethink how he spends his time. The road of reconnecting with his daughter, restoring his marriage, and rekindling old friendships may be long and complex, but it is worthwhile. Relationships, after all, make our life truly meaningful, enhancing our existence in ways that no 'winnable game' can.

Edwin's Story:

Now an adult, Edwin studied the threads of connection or lack thereof that distinguished his early years. His father had been an ever-present yet aloof figure in his life. His father's life was mostly consumed with work as a foreman at a construction company, leaving little room for anything else, including building meaningful ties with his family.

Edwin remembered his father as a guy in motion, either leaving for work or returning tired from a long day at the building site. His father's strength was apparent, as was his intense devotion to providing for his family, but Edwin couldn't help but feel that there was a missing piece of the picture.

The man he knew as his father was a provider rather than a parent. Edwin remembered his father returning home, his work boots leaving dust trails behind him, his face set in a permanent frown of tiredness and tension. He would have given everything for a pat on the back, a shared chuckle, or a bedtime story. Most days, though, his father was too weary or engrossed with thoughts of the next day's work.

Edwin became more aware of this pattern as he grew older, in his connection with his father and other aspects of his life. Unknowingly, his father had set a precedent for him. Like his father, Edwin struggled as an adult to establish and sustain connections. He recognized his behavior mirrored his father's - always putting work first, often at the price of personal relationships.

Like his father's, his relationships began to resemble professional assignments - something to be handled rather than treasured. He found himself putting his energy where he felt most needed - at business, networking events, and meetings - but lacked the time and emotional bandwidth to nurture the relationships that mattered to him. His father's influence substantially affected his perspective, and he could see its impact on his attitude to relationships. Edwin found himself in a constant battle as he progressed in life, attempting to reconcile his professional commitments with his connections, a problem he was all too acquainted with.

Edwin understood that the shadow of his father's work-focused lifestyle had severely impacted on his experiences as he followed the track of his life. This wasn't just a hazy childhood memory but a story that had become entwined with the fabric of his adult life.

Edwin was a natural leader at work, a go-getter who knew how to get things done. He had picked up these characteristics from his father, who had diligently navigated the complex world of construction projects. His coworkers liked his enthusiasm and commitment and frequently praised his work ethic. When the office lights went out and the clamor of the workweek died away, Edwin found himself wandering into an uncomfortable silence.

Edwin often felt like a ship at sea in his personal life. His relationship seemed to slide away, just out of reach. He could feel the distance widening but didn't know how to bridge it. His friendships included missed birthdays, hasty phone calls, and sporadic meetings. His romantic relationships frequently began with a spark but died out due to his incapacity to commit the time and emotional energy required to keep the flame alive.

Edwin also observed that this habit was harming not only his relationships with others but also his relationship with himself. His sense of self, which had formerly been dynamic and complex, appeared to be shrinking to his professional identity. He was more than his profession, but he struggled to connect with the other components of his identity. His hobbies and interests took a back seat while work took center stage, leaving him feeling empty.

His memories of his father were a sobering reminder of the implications of a life dominated by work. He could see his father's face carved with tired wrinkles, his eyes reflecting the fatigue of a life devoted to service to work. Despite his father's success, Edwin couldn't help but wonder if the cost of lost connections and strained relationships was worth it.

Edwin was trapped in a loop. A narrative passed down to him. The difficulties he had in forming and keeping relationships reflected the lifestyle he had observed and, to a significant part, assimilated. His father's world had become his own, and he lived in the echoes of a past defined by work and the sacrifices it demanded.

Edwin's decision needed to be more straightforward. It required an inner adjustment, a profound reevaluation of what he valued most. He found himself at a crossroads, a transition point where he needed to modify his ways consciously. The path of least resistance would have been to continue on his current course, gaining professional awards as his connections deteriorated. But Edwin recognized he wanted more and decided to devote time to sustaining his ties with his family and friends.

This decision came with its difficulties. Balancing hard work with personal commitments was like walking a tightrope. He had to learn to say no, delegate, prioritize, and, most importantly, take time for himself and the people who were most important to him. There were days when he stumbled when the guilt of missing a deadline or the worry of missing out on a career change weighed heavy on him. But each time, he reminded himself of his decision and his commitment to the people he cared about.

The change occurred gradually. Changes did not happen overnight. But with every passing day, Edwin observed a change. No longer were conversations with friends and family hurried or superficial. He began to appreciate the pleasure of a shared chuckle and the solace of a familiar voice. He began to value the profound satisfaction that comes from nurturing a relationship and the sense of belonging that comes from being a member of a community, family, or group of peers.

He also observed that his relationships were intensifying. His friends and family shared more of their fears, aspirations, and ambitions with him. Edwin found himself similarly articulating his emotions, concerns, and aspirations. He realized that, like flora, relationships require care to flourish. They need time, consideration, and respect. And he was willing to provide them in great quantity.

Edwin's existence was no longer exclusively defined by his professional accomplishments. His extensive relationships added color, substance, and significance to his life. The void he had felt was steadily filled, not with accolades and achievements, but with love, comprehension, and a sense of belonging.

Edwin's voyage still needed to be completed. He knew there would be obstacles along the path, times when he would be tested and fail. However, he also knew that he had invested in the people he adored and placed relationships above personal gain. He was determined to adhere to his decision, no matter what.

Sharon's Story:

Once full of passion and energy, Sharon's life was controlled for a long time by the quest for financial riches and societal position. Living in a society marked by materialism and consumerism, she became entangled in the never-ending pursuit of wealth. Like many others, she was captivated by the enticing lifestyles portrayed in TV shows and social media. The possibility of fast earning fortune with little effort was too appealing. She was, however, completely unaware that this pursuit would come at a high cost.

For many years, her only goal was to provide a nice living for her family. She convinced herself that her prominent role as a wife and mother was to provide for the family. She and her husband, who had formerly enjoyed a profound and passionate bond, began to drift away over time. Their chats became less regular, and their shared times became more scarce. Sharon was so preoccupied with accumulating worldly wealth that she ignored their growing distance.

Surprisingly, while she worked tirelessly to provide a decent life for her family, the essential core of their relationship was collapsing. Her husband was becoming increasingly isolated and unnoticed. He desired quality time with the woman he had been in love with for over ten years, not financial stuff. Sharon realized that her pursuit of fortune had cost her the exact thing she was trying to care for - her family.

This discovery had a great impact on her. She began to doubt her decisions and the priorities she had established. She began to recognize the importance of fostering relationships and devoting time and attention to their upkeep. She realized that life is about more than simply making relationships; it is also about keeping them.

She realized she was not alone in her challenges through women's organizations, conferences, and leadership coaching sessions. Many others offered similar stories about balancing three crucial areas of life: God, family and friends, and career. It was a delicate balancing act that required careful time and priority management.

Unfortunately, her awakening came a little late. Her marriage, which had been ignored for far too long, was annulled. The pain and anguish were a sharp reminder of the costs of failing to maintain relationships. The hole created by her husband's disappearance was a bitter reminder of the price she had paid for her quest for financial wealth.

However, this traumatic encounter served as a watershed moment. It taught her the value of having a sense of balance in her life. **Her new priorities included:**

- Spending time with God.
- Cultivating relationships with family and friends.
- Devoting herself to her job.
- It was a difficult shift but vital for living an entire life.

In reflection, she admits her errors. Her experience is typical. It's a cautionary tale about the cost of ignoring one's relationships in pursuit of material gain. It serves as a reminder that, while money might be comforting, our connections enhance our lives. Ultimately, the key to a happy life is not material stuff but the quality of our relationships, love, and camaraderie with our loved ones.

We may feel more isolated than ever in an increasingly computerized and connected world. With our attention continually tugged in a million different directions, from job to parenting to maintaining a social life, it's easy to lose sight of the value of developing and nourishing our relationships. Despite technological developments, we are frequently left feeling lonely and alienated.

Something needs to change. We must return to the underlying human urge for connection and belonging. We bring you "Inclusive Bonds - The Web of Connections: A Comprehensive Plan for Building and Maintaining Relationships" to assist us in navigating this complicated web of ties. This solution is intended to offer you the skills and techniques you need to establish and sustain strong, meaningful friendships throughout time.

This all-encompassing plan considers all parts of your life, from your family and friends to your profession and spiritual path. It tries to assist you in balancing these diverse aspects so you can live a meaningful and enriching life. Following this method will teach you not only how to make connections but also how to keep them. The Web of Connections is more than a plan; it's a road to a more connected and enriched life.

"Prioritize Your Relationships" is the first step.

a. **Identify Key Relationships:** To begin, you must identify the connections in your life that are most essential to you. These should be with God (first and foremost), your family, friends, co-workers, or a spiritual community such as church or groups. Begin by listing the people who mean the most to you.

b. **Assess Your Time Investment:** Consider how much time you spend with these people. Are there some people you rarely communicate with despite their importance to you? Do you spend much time with people, yet the relationship could be more rewarding than it is?

c. **Create a Relationship Goal:** Establish a clear aim for each crucial relationship. "Spend 15 minutes every morning reading the Bible (God's Word), another 10 minutes meditating on what you just read, and 5 minutes of prayer to begin your day," for example. "Spend at least one-on-one time with each of my children at least once a week," for example, or "Have a date night with my spouse every two weeks."

d. **Schedule Time for Your Relationships:** Now that you have goals, it's time to implement them. This could include scheduling a coffee date with a friend every Saturday morning or taking a half-day off work monthly to spend with your partner.

e. **Consistency is Key:** Prioritizing relationships is a continuous process that demands consistent effort. Make it a habit to evaluate your goals and plan frequently to stay on track.
f. **Quality Over Quantity:** It's not so much about how much time you spend as it is about the quality of that time. Even small moments of genuine connection can significantly impact your relationships.

"Regular Communication" is the second step.

a. **Establish a Routine:** Consistent communication does not happen by chance. You'll need to develop a process for checking in with key people frequently. Depending on the nature of the connection, this could be done daily, weekly, or monthly.
b. **Choose Your Medium:** Not every communication must be done face-to-face. Among the options are phone calls, text messaging, video chats, emails, and handwritten letters. Select the strategy that works best for both you and the other person.
c. **Active Listening:** Effective communication involves more than just talking; it also involves listening. When conversing with someone, make an effort to listen actively. This includes hearing their words and observing their emotions and nonverbal signs.
d. **Express Yourself:** Don't hesitate to express your opinions and thoughts. Building solid relationships requires open and honest communication.
e. **Ask Open-Ended Questions:** One of the most effective techniques to promote communication is to ask open-ended questions. These questions take more thought and discussion than a simple 'yes' or 'no' answer.
f. **Respect Differences:** Because people have varied communication styles, it is crucial to identify these variances. Try to match the other person's communication style and be patient if they communicate differently.

 g. Stay Positive: Positive communication is more likely to result in a positive connection. Maintain a pleasant tone in your communication by focusing on the positive and expressing thanks.

Keep in mind that communication is the lifeblood of any relationship. Regular, open, and honest communication will help you understand and connect with the people who are important to you.

"Demonstrate Appreciation" is the third step.

 a. Say "Thank You" Often: It may appear simple, but expressing thanks regularly can make a significant difference. Don't take other people's acts for granted. Tell them how much you appreciate their efforts, no matter how minor.
 b. Show Recognition: Acknowledge the accomplishments and milestones of folks in your relationship network. Make them feel unique by celebrating their achievements.
 c. Give Compliments: Genuine compliments can help others feel valued. Take note of the small details; don't be afraid to share your admiration.
 d. Give Small Gifts: Thank-you gifts do not have to be extravagant. Small, thoughtful gifts can be equally, if not more, significant.
 e. Spend Quality Time: One of the most valuable presents you can give someone is your time. Spend quality time with individuals you value to show them how much they matter to you.

Remember that everyone wishes to be appreciated. It is a beautiful way to build relationships and express gratitude to people.

"Embrace Open and Honest Communication" is the fourth step.

a. **Foster a Safe Space:** Ensure that the people in your connection network feel safe expressing their opinions and feelings without fear of being judged or retaliated against.
b. **Express Yourself Clearly:** Be honest about your feelings and thoughts. Avoid ambiguity by communicating in an easy-to-understand manner.
c. **Practice Non-Violent Communication:** Use nonviolent communication when dealing with conflicts or sensitive themes. This entails communicating your wants and feelings without blaming or condemning the other person.
d. **Use "I" Statements:** Instead of beginning sentences with "You," which might come across as accusatory, use "I" statements to explain how you feel or what you require.

Any strong relationship is built on open and honest communication. Increase communication within your relationship network and make it by following these methods.

"Gift of Presence" is the fifth step.

a. **Disconnect to Connect:** Keep Distractions to a Minimum. Put your phone away, switch off the TV, and avoid distractions when you're with someone. This enables you to give them your undivided attention.
b. **The Eye Contact Connection:** Maintain Eye Contact. Eye contact indicates paying attention to the person and the discourse. It's an effective method to demonstrate your engagement and interest.
c. **Mindful Moments:** Develop your mindfulness skills. Being mindful entails being present in the current moment. Stay engaged in the experience while you're with someone, focusing on the discussion and how you feel.

    d. **Responsive Reactions:** Demonstrate Engagement through Responses. React correctly to the conversation. Whether it's laughter at a joke, a thoughtful nod, or a pertinent inquiry, your reactions demonstrate that you're interested and attentive.

    e. **Sharing the Spotlight:** Ensure Equal Participation. Encourage the other individual to speak up and share their feelings. Ensure the conversation isn't one-sided, and everyone gets their moment in the spotlight.

    f. **Recall and Relate:** Remember and Refer to Previous Conversations. Remembering information from previous talks and bringing them up later demonstrates that you listened and cared about the individual and your relationship.

Practicing these tips can help you be more present and engaged in your relationships, demonstrating to others that you truly value your time together.

"The Nurturing Touch" is the sixth step.

    a. **Express to Impress:** Express Your Emotions. Tell the individuals in your life how much you appreciate them. Openly express your love, admiration, or respect for them. These affirmations can aid in the nurturing and strengthening of your relationships.

    b. **Small Acts, Big Impacts:** Demonstrate kindness through your actions. Small acts of kindness can make a tremendous difference. This might be as simple as bringing your partner a cup of tea, assisting a colleague with a demanding job, or calling a friend to check-in.

    c. **Surprise and Delight:** Plan unexpected gestures. Surprises can liven up your relationships. This might be a romantic date, a meaningful present, or a handwritten message left for them to discover.

    d. **Thick and Thin:** Be Present in Tough Times. It is critical to show support at difficult times. Your presence may make a tremendous impact, whether as a shoulder to weep on, counsel when asked for, or simply being there to listen.

Regularly nurturing your connections allows them to thrive and grow, making your links solid and meaningful.

Sailing Through Storms "Manage Conflicts Healthily" is the 7th step.

a. **Calm Over Storm:** Maintain Emotional Control During a Storm. In a quarrel, avoid reacting rashly. Even if the other person is upset, stay calm and composed. This can help to keep the condition from worsening.

b. **Understanding, Not Winning:** Strive for resolution rather than victory. In any debate, your goal should be to reach an agreement rather than to "win" the argument. Rather than fostering bitterness and hostility, this worldview develops respect and understanding.

c. **The Blame Game:** Avoid pointing the finger at the other person. Instead, concentrate on communicating your relationship's sentiments and requirements. Instead of "You always.", use "I" phrases like "I feel upset when…"

d. **Listen to Learn:** Practice Active Listening. Active listening is essential, even during a fight. Listen to the other person's point of view and feelings without interruption. This can help you comprehend their point of view and validate their feelings.

e. **Seek the Source:** Identify the Root Cause. Conflicts are frequently the result of deeper concerns. Determine the issue at the heart of the debate, which may or may not be the original topic of the discussion.

f. **Find a Fair Fix:** Offer Constructive Solutions. Work together to create a solution that satisfies both sides after understanding each other's perspectives. This could entail making a concession or trying a new method you hadn't considered before.

g. **Seeds of Forgiveness:** Apologize and Forgive. If you've offended someone, honestly apologize. Also, if you've been injured, be willing to forgive them. Holding grudges can be detrimental to a relationship in the long run.

Healthy dispute resolution can strengthen your relationships by showing mutual respect and a desire to understand and meet each other's needs.

"Building Bridges" - Reconnect and Rebuild is the 8th and final step.

a. **First Step Forward:** Take the Initiative. Don't wait for the other person to initiate contact. Send them a message or phone them. Your initiative could be the spark that sparks the relationship back to life.
b. **Sincerity Speaks:** Make Your Intentions Clear. Be upfront about your want to reconnect. This demonstrates your Sincerity and commitment to healing the connection.
c. **A Trip Down Memory Lane:** Shared Experiences. Remind them of the pleasant experiences you had together. This can help to reawaken positive emotions and remind both of you why the relationship is worth fixing.
d. **Apologies and Amend:** If necessary, apologize. If the connection has suffered due to a misunderstanding or a mistake, express your honest regret. Accepting responsibility for one's conduct might pave the way for forgiveness and healing.
e. **The Forgotten Chapters:** Discover What Went Wrong. Try to figure out what caused the break in your relationship. This may entail awkward conversations, but understanding the past is critical to avoid making the same mistakes.
f. **Fresh Pages:** Begin with a Blank Slate. Once you've grasped the past, aim to start over. Let go of any lingering bitterness or negativity and concentrate on repairing your connection healthily.

g. **Steady Steps:** Be patient and consistent. It takes time to rebuild a relationship. Be patient, and continuously demonstrate your dedication to the partnership. Regular conversation, understanding, and concern can gradually restore trust and connection.

It is challenging to rebuild a relationship, but it is worthwhile when it comes to meaningful ties in your life.

Our journey through the complexities of human connection leads us to conclude that nurturing and growing meaningful relationships is an art that can only be honed with time, effort, and a lot of heart. The foundation of this art is a single word, a modest hello, yet it is the powerful initiator of many conversations and connections that shape the direction of our life. A simple, heartfelt "Hello" can do wonders.

Simply saying "hello" can open a world of possibilities and only takes a second of your time. It's an open invitation to enter another person's life and gain insight, knowledge, and a sense of belonging. As we close this book, we want to use "The Power of Hello" to our advantage, as this simple greeting can pave the way for a genuine connection that may last a lifetime.

"The Power of Hello" - Initiating a Relationship:

a. **Initiate with Ease:** A simple greeting. Never underestimate the effectiveness of a simple "Hello." It's the initial step in starting a discussion and expressing interest, and it can lead to the start of a beautiful relationship.

b. **Warmth in Words:** Be sincere and friendly when you greet someone. Because your tone and body language may set the tone for the entire discussion, ensure they are nice and open.

c. **Body Language Speaks:** Practice Open Body Language. Non-verbal indicators can have a significant impact on how friendly you appear. Maintain eye contact, face the person you are conversing with, and keep your arms uncrossed. This body language conveys openness and readiness to participate.

d. **Reveal Interest:** Show Your Interest. Building a relationship requires expressing interest in the other person's thoughts, feelings, and experiences. This could be asking about their day, interests, or opinions on a specific topic.

e. **Respectful Consistency:** Always be respectful and interested. The impact of a greeting continues after the first meeting. Always greet them warmly, show genuine interest in them, and respect them. This frequent, pleasant engagement might lay the groundwork for a solid relationship.

f. **Transcend Hello:** Transcend Greetings are no longer sufficient. Conversations should extend beyond simple welcomes as your friendship develops. Dive further into debates, offer personal experiences, and demonstrate empathy. This will help you better understand each other and deepen your relationship.

g. **Express Intent:** Be Clear About Your Intentions. If you're romantically interested in them or wish to strengthen your connection with them, it might be good to say this at some point. Be direct, respectful, and aware that they may or may not share your feelings.

h. **Respect Boundaries:** Be considerate of others' personal space. When interacting with others, keep a polite distance. Invading someone's personal space may make you appear unapproachable.

i. **Open Up:** Tell Us About Yourself. Being honest about your feelings and experiences will help you become more approachable. Sharing makes others feel more connected to you and encourages them to open up in return.

j. **Accessible Attitude:** Be easily accessible. Strive to be accessible by swiftly returning calls and messages or being available for conversations. An approachable person is accessible and responsive.

k. **Patience and Persistence:** Allow Time for the Relationship to Grow. It takes time to develop a meaningful relationship. Be patient and allow the relationship to develop naturally. Continue your efforts, but make sure they are welcomed and reciprocated.

By adopting transparency, you make yourself approachable and provide the groundwork for trust and understanding, essential in every lasting relationship.

As we close this chapter on "The LIGHT Pathway" Inclusive Bond, I hope you've gained valuable insights into the intricate web of relationships and the importance of nurturing them. The steps provided are designed to help you establish and maintain strong, healthy bonds with the people in your life, fostering a network of connections that are fulfilling, supportive, and enriching. Remember, the journey towards maintaining these bonds is continuous, and the effort you invest today will reap benefits in the long run.

As we venture forth, we approach the third gate, preparing to explore the concept of "Generous Empathy - The Oasis." This is a place of sanctuary in the middle of your journey, a place to cultivate a spirit of empathy and compassion. As you delve into the art of understanding, you embark on a journey of self-discovery and acknowledgment of others' experiences.

This stage is about fostering generosity of spirit, enabling you to look beyond the surface-level biases, stereotypes, or worldviews that may hinder wholesome interactions. Doing so paves the way for deeper connections enriched by empathy and understanding. An oasis is a place of growth and transformation where you learn to view the world and its inhabitants compassionately. This is about understanding others and better understanding yourself, your responses, and your approach to the world.

So, brace yourself as we embark on this next chapter of our journey. As you walk through the third gate, remember that every step you take is a step closer to realizing the profound impact you can have on your life and the lives of others when you choose to walk the path of empathy and understanding. Onward, to the Oasis.

Chapter 10

Generous Empathy - The Oasis (Developing compassion and understanding)

Being immersed in the tranquil waters of "Generous Empathy - The Oasis" brings into sharp focus the extent to which our fates are interwoven. Every person we encounter has their background, experiences, and struggles. To connect with others and manage our relationships well, we must first recognize the complexity of the human condition.

Understanding the motivations behind another person's thoughts and feelings is a key component of empathy. Being empathetic and open-hearted improves our abilities as listeners, communicators, and supporters. We adjust our mindset, viewing conflict less as a competition to be won and more as an opportunity to grow as individuals and as a community.

Here at Oasis, we learn to examine issues from several vantage points. This is more than an attempt to put oneself in another person's shoes. Understanding their background, customs, and lifestyle is crucial. We recognize that our experiences and those around us influence the lens through which we view the world. Understanding and respecting these differences helps us become better individuals.

Self-discovery is an integral part of this journey. Taking an introspective look at oneself helps one understand other people better. Our deepest motivations, beliefs, and biases are explored. Through introspection, we gain insight into our strengths and weaknesses, emotional triggers, and behavioral patterns. This kind of self-awareness is crucial because it allows us to interact with people constructively rather than defensively and to learn from them rather than judge them.

Developing this kind of compassion broadens our perspective, helping us to see past our preconceived notions and connect with others on a more human level despite our differences. This outlook in life broadens one's horizons and adds depth to one's relationships. As a result, our connections with others will improve and flourish.

In this chapter, you will learn specific strategies for cultivating such deep empathy, managing your relationships with maturity and compassion, and embarking on a journey of discovery. Remember that with each step we take and our revelation, we advance in wisdom, compassion, and solidarity as we discover more of Oasis. Let's get started on the path toward deeper relationships and more selfless compassion. Here in the Oasis, everything is simple.

Today, our positive and unpleasant Oasis experiences are heavily influenced by our worldviews and the use of social media.

One positive effect of social media and diverse points of view is that they broaden our exposure to new ideas and ways of thinking. They can help us learn to empathize with others from other backgrounds by enlightening us about different cultures, methods of living, and ways of thinking. They can assist in promoting global empathy and unity by easing communication and connection across national and cultural boundaries.

However, we should be wary of the echo chambers that these platforms and viewpoints can foster, where we only hear voices that reflect our own and lose the ability to understand and empathize with individuals with different beliefs. They can also add to the problem of information overload that leaves us feeling drained and alienated.

As we travel through the Oasis, we come to a decision point. The city of Social Media, full of lively activity, various voices, and unlimited data, can be found down one road. It's a metropolis that never rests, buzzing with the excitement of new information, photos, memes, and challenges. It allows us to communicate with people worldwide, share our ideas and opinions, and gain insight into other societies and worldviews.

As we explore further, we become aware of the darkness behind the city's shiny veneer. The city's buildings planned to use advanced algorithms, all tend to make us feel at ease and at home. Our opinions and tastes are reflected in the streets, and we live in a safe little bubble called an echo chamber. There is little opportunity for disagreement or alternative viewpoints within these chambers since our ideas are magnified and reinforced. The city's design gradually promotes polarization, lowering residents' ability to empathize with individuals with different views.

We find ourselves at the city's bazaar, a veritable treasure trove of knowledge. However, we can see stands selling fabricated goods alongside the real deal. The market's breadth and the transactions' rapidity make it hard to tell reality from fantasy. Misinformation is ubiquitous, clouding our judgment, fueling prejudice, and preventing us from understanding others.

Further exploration leads us to a distressing sight: stadiums where people, shielded by the city's anonymity, put on a disturbing exhibition of depersonalization and dehumanization for the benefit of an audience. Cyberbullying and trolling flourish due to the emotional distance established by the city's digital character.

Our city exploration has bright spots, but the darkness obscures them. There are serious risks to our mental health if we constantly compare ourselves to others' highlight reels, avoid face-to-face contact, and isolate ourselves.

However, despite living in the "social media city," we are not helpless. We can learn how to handle it maturely, with consideration and compassion. We can stop talking to ourselves, seek alternative perspectives, and confront our prejudices. We have the option of investigating and verifying material before passing it along. We can fight against the dehumanization and personalization of the internet by treating people with the same kindness and compassion as in person. We can maintain our capacity for empathy by striking a balance between time spent in the city and in person. More significantly, we can take care of our mental health by acknowledging when we need to take a break from the hustle and bustle of daily life and find peace elsewhere.

As we travel through the Oasis, we understand that empathy and compassion require not just putting ourselves in the position of another person but also learning to recognize and negotiate the social and technological environments that affect our perspectives and relationships. Through study and development, we actively work to foster a culture of generous empathy. We go closer to achieving harmony, compassion, and self-awareness with every step.

Greg's Story:

In his hometown of central Wisconsin, Greg worked as a mechanic. The hum of the engines he maintained, the filth of his coworkers, and the trust of the regulars who came to him for advice all soothed him. The people and places in his life wove together in comfortable patterns.

Greg, though, felt he needed to improve. He desired to see the world outside his native country and become familiar with cultures, customs, and views unlike his own. The promise of near-instantaneous interaction lured him in. He came into this world expecting great things and prepared to develop and improve.

The power of social networking initially took Greg aback. He had access to other vehicle enthusiasts, professionals in many disciplines, and debates about current events worldwide. It seemed like you were in a massive, bustling city where you could always meet and learn from new people.

But the more Greg researched, the more he discovered the city's dark side. As his in-person interactions were reduced, he became addicted to the screen and spent more and more time online. His once-cherished routine had been displaced by the constant urge to check updates, respond to comments, and engage in intense online debates. His life seemed to lose all significance and vigor when he was not connected to the internet.

Greg was also beginning to feel a rising sense of inferiority and discontent. Every time he logged in, he was greeted with posts from pals who appeared to be enjoying picture-perfect lives full of thrilling new adventures that contrasted sharply with his own. His previously prosperous life began to feel hollow, and his achievements became meaningless.

Greg was profoundly affected by an online debate on the environment. An educated discussion quickly deteriorated into personal attacks on Greg due to his lack of education. He felt mocked, abused, and strangely alone in the big internet city.

Greg's life changed dramatically as a result of this. His mental health, relationships, and overall quality of life were all suffering due to his excessive use of social media. Greg attempted to change his perspective on social media to retake control.

He started by arranging social media time at specific times of day and then keeping to that schedule. He returned to his hobbies and discovered fresh joy in engaging with others in the real world. He began to appreciate the depth and authenticity of in-person interactions with those around him.

Greg shunned toxic people and content in favor of accounts that supplied him with helpful information and motivation. He had to keep reminding himself that the reality portrayed on social media was manipulated and should not be used as a yardstick.

Greg had a difficult time on this vacation. He struggled with withdrawal, fear of missing out, and relapse. He eventually figured out how to navigate the social media metropolis without feeling bewildered. The Oasis meant more to him than just remaining in contact with the outside world; it also meant taking care of himself.

Trials and difficulties marked Greg's stay at the Oasis, but ultimately triumph and development. His ups and downs have shaped him into someone who can navigate the dangerous seas of social media without losing sight of who he is or his ability to feel sympathy for others. On his path, each day brings new challenges, learning opportunities, and opportunities for progress.

Jeff's Story:

In the late 1990s, a young and ambitious computer programmer named Jeff stood on the verge of joining the Oasis. He'd fallen for Ana, a vibrant and kind nurse at the local hospital. However, there was a stumbling block: Jeff was a white man, and Ana was a black woman. Interracial partnerships were less widespread then and frequently met with public confusion or rejection.

Jeff sought guidance from a close friend one day when anxiety and doubt clouded his head. He expressed his concerns regarding potential cultural differences and preconceptions. His friend's remarks hit home: "What matters is that she treats you right, and you share the same values, or can at least compromise." The most significant point is who cares what people say, even your family, which is against interracial relationships.

Jeff chose to accept his journey through the Oasis after hearing these words. He married Ana, and they faced the difficulties of social stereotypes and biases together. These trials were challenging, but their friendship, founded on mutual understanding, respect, and love, remained strong.

Their trip through the Oasis took on additional dimensions when they started a family. Their children, born into a broad cultural mix, provided them with various worldviews. This diversity, however, presented its own set of issues. Cultural traditions occasionally clashed, and extended family members had differing expectations.

Nonetheless, Jeff saw these as opportunities for growth and learning rather than hurdles. He taught his children to value their cultural heritage and be proud of their blended ancestry. Discussions on identity and culture were regular in their home, and questions were always encouraged and explored.

Jeff exhibited what it means to challenge cultural assumptions and biases through his behavior. He taught his children that love was about embracing and celebrating differences rather than fearing them. His children internalized these principles, molding them into compassionate people capable of navigating their Oasis with grace and understanding.

More than twenty years later, Jeff and Ana remain happily married. Their children, now adults, apply lessons from their parents in their lives and communities. Their family, a beautiful blend of cultures, is a testament to Jeff's journey through the Oasis.

In retrospect, Jeff feels nothing but gratitude for his journey through the Oasis. What once seemed like a place of fear and uncertainty became a sanctuary for growth and transformation. His experiences have profoundly shaped him, his relationships, and his family. As he reflects on his journey, he is forever grateful for the Oasis and its teachings.

As the years went by, Jeff's journey through the Oasis continued. His work as a computer programmer brought new challenges, while his family life was filled with unique joys and struggles. His relationship with Ana remained a constant source of love and support, but they, too, had to navigate the ebbs and flows of life together.

One day, Jeff found himself faced with a significant professional challenge. His company was undergoing a major restructuring, and as a result, he was tasked with leading a diverse team of programmers, some of whom hailed from different parts of the world. This diversity brought a rich blend of perspectives and skills to the team but came with the challenge of overcoming language barriers and cultural differences.

Remembering his experiences in the Oasis, Jeff decided to approach this challenge with empathy and understanding. He tried to learn about his team members' cultures and even picked up a few phrases in their languages. He facilitated open discussions where team members could share their perspectives and ideas, fostering an inclusive environment where everyone felt heard and valued.

In his personal life, Jeff continued to grow alongside Ana. They navigated the challenges of raising their children into adulthood, supporting them as they began to forge their paths. The values of empathy and understanding that Jeff and Ana had instilled in their children became evident as they grew into compassionate, open-minded individuals.

As Jeff and Ana became empty nesters, they found themselves at a new stage in their journey through the Oasis. With more time for each other, they deepened their relationship, exploring new hobbies and activities together. They traveled, learning about different cultures and expanding their horizons. These experiences further enriched their understanding of each other and the world around them.

Jeff sees a path filled with development, understanding, and love as he reflects on his journey through the Oasis. Each challenge he faced, whether professionally or personally, served as an opportunity for him to deepen his empathy and compassion. His journey taught him that true strength lies in avoiding and facing difficulties with an open heart and mind.

Jeff's journey through the Oasis is far from over. As he moves forward, he continues cultivating his spirit of empathy and understanding, guided by the knowledge that every experience is an opportunity for growth. His story is a testament to the Oasis's transformative power, a sanctuary fostering compassion, unity, and self-discovery.

As we journey together through the Oasis, let us embrace this transformative process with open hearts and minds. To aid us in this journey, and harness the power of the Oasis, **here are step-by-step instructions with examples for each of the five magical steps:**

1. Digital Detox - 'Magic Hour'

   Step 1: Choose an hour free from daily obligations and distractions. This could be early in the morning, during lunch, or before bed.

   Step 2: Turn off all electronic devices and put them in a different room.

   Step 3: Engage in an activity that brings you joy. This could be reading your favorite fantasy novel, painting a watercolor landscape, or taking a peaceful walk-in nature.

Example: If you choose the morning, you could use this time to practice yoga, followed by a mindful breakfast where you pay attention to every bite.

2. Escape the Echo Chamber - 'Perspective Passport'

   Step 1: Choose a day each week for exploration.

   Step 2: Pick a topic or culture different from your own. This could be a political viewpoint, a foreign culture, or a scientific field.

   Step 3: Dive in! Read articles, watch documentaries, or have discussions about the chosen topic.

Example: If you're interested in Japanese culture, you could watch a documentary about Japanese tea ceremonies, try making sushi, or read a book by a Japanese author.

3. **Mindful Engagement - 'Present Presence'**

   Step 1: When you're having a conversation, remind yourself to stay present.

   Step 2: Imagine your 'Presence Meter.' This meter fills up when you focus
completely on the other person and their viewpoint.

   Step 3: Keep the meter full during the conversation. If your mind wanders, gently bring it back.

Example: If you're talking to a friend about their day, focus solely on their words, emotions, and body language. If you find your mind wandering to your to-do list, gently redirect your attention to your friend.

4. **Empathy Exercises - 'Walk in Their Shoes.'**

   Step 1: Identify a situation where you experienced a conflict or misunderstanding with someone.
   Example: A colleague missed a deadline for a project you're both working on.

   Step 2: Reflect on the situation from the other person's perspective. Try to understand their possible feelings and thoughts.
   Example: Instead of reacting with annoyance, consider your colleague's circumstances. Could they be dealing with personal issues or a heavy workload?

   Step 3: Write down the thoughts and feelings you believe the other person might have experienced.

Example: "My colleague might be feeling stressed due to personal issues. They might be worried about the consequences of missing the deadline."

5. Empathy-Boosting Activities - 'Empathy Elixir'

Step 1: Identify activities that increase your empathy.

Step 2: Regularly engage in these activities.

Step 3: Reflect on how these activities enhance your understanding of others.

Example: You could read a book from the perspective of a character unlike yourself, volunteer at a local homeless shelter, or serve at a church that always needs volunteers. After each activity, reflect on how it has helped you understand other people's experiences.

Accepting these magical steps can assist you in navigating the difficulties of our interconnected environment. Remember that the goal isn't to immediately become flawless at understanding and empathizing with everyone around you. Instead, it is about embarking on a steady path of self-discovery and growth. As you follow these steps, your world will grow, your connections will deepen, and your perspective will become refined. Allow the magic to happen in your life, and watch as you develop a deeper connection with yourself and others.

As we wrap up this chapter, please take a moment to reflect on the adventure we've had together. We've arrived at the Oasis from the parched desert, a haven of nutrition and refreshment where we've developed great empathy and cemented our relationships. However, this is merely the beginning of our transformational path.

The stage is now set for our next chapter, "Harmonious Evolution: The Transition." This stage is a watershed moment: the abstract becomes tangible, and intentions become actions. It is an active change phase, transitioning from entrenched behaviors and damaging worldviews to a more balanced, fulfilling life.

We are not the same people we were when we entered the Oasis. We now have a better grasp of empathy and a more robust network of ties. These are takeaways and tools that will help us make positive life changes.

The ideas we've gained from God's Word and insights from our relationships will be applied to our lives in the next chapter. We'll start by changing the areas of our lives that we've identified as harmful or impeding our progress and replace them with healthier, more positive alternatives.

Prepare to enter a period of imagining and implementing transformation - a period in which visions take shape and goals become a reality. The shift will not be simple; it will necessitate tenacity, commitment, and trust in oneself. Nonetheless, the advantages are enormous.

So, let us prepare to embark on this new chapter to begin our journey on the next part of "The LIGHT Pathway," the Harmonious Evolution. The trip continues, as does our development. Prepare yourself for the beautiful transition that is about to occur.

Chapter 11

Harmonious Evolution - The Transition (Envisioning and implementing change)

Like a river that has finally made it through the mountains and is hungry to flow into the sea and become a part of something bigger, we are on the cusp of transformation, about to start on the magnificent trip known as "Harmonious Evolution: The Transition."

So far, we've prevailed in the hospitable Oasis of mutual understanding and support. We have reached a juncture where our moral compass indicates a choice must be made. Our joint development depends on our ability to fill in the blanks of an uncharted future.

The first phase of our plan to achieve our objective is detailed below. This goal is more than an end; it is the impetus for our efforts. It's a beacon that helps us see our way through the night and across the waves of transition and unpredictability.

Along this road, we will encounter the winds of transformation and the waves that remake our lives. We acknowledge the difficulty and significance of adjusting to novel conditions. This instrument is the chisel that carves our identities and directs our growth.

Our journey was inspired by the compassion we had developed at the Oasis. It's a map that shows us the way across the complex landscape of human feelings and viewpoints. It's a way to broaden one's social circle and intellectual perspectives by listening to the experiences of others.

Our growth is more of a whirlwind of action, introspection, and transformation than a steady ascent. We try things out with some uncertainty, evaluate the outcomes, and modify our approach accordingly. It's a twirling dance that keeps us on course and energized, and with each revolution, we move closer to our goal.

In the end, our travels shape our routines in novel ways. They keep us solid through life's ups and downs and rooted in the future we see. These routines keep us from reverting to old ways of doing things and allow us to keep our focus on our objectives.

We shall be significantly aided on our journey by the wisdom revealed in God's Word and the connections we have made. They act as sails, catching the winds of change and carrying us forward following the laws of nature, welcoming you to "The Transition" when our plan takes shape and our fate is first determined. Change and growth happen here. In the end, we shape up to be like this.

Despite the chaos, a beacon of hope remains. As we approach The Transition, we know peace can only be achieved through conflict. We hone our ability to discern the subtle distinctions between truth and deceit. Our goal is to use the power of critical thinking to shine a light on the murky world of social media and shed some light on the reasons for various societal chess moves. We aim to transform the group into a harmonizing choir where everyone's voice is heard and valued. This struggle and effort are vital to our journey and fundamental to our peaceful development.

The media of our time—television, movies, and the internet—tell stories about our collective experience of the world. The problem is that these stories often have subtexts that subtly (and sometimes overtly) impact our attitudes, beliefs, and actions.

Sensationalism and bias in the media can distort our view of the world, fostering the growth of prejudice and ensuring the persistence of existing barriers. Cultivating seeds of conflict rather than understanding and empathy can slow our efforts to achieve more sustainable development.

Movies significantly affect culture because of the dramatic stories they tell and how they portray reality. Myths can be busted, people can be inspired to take action, and deep discussions can be initiated. Yet they carry the risk of normalizing lousy behavior, disseminating incorrect notions, and romanticizing harmful strife. This conflict can propel us forward in the quest for a more harmonious society or hold us back.

There are benefits and drawbacks to today's digital public squares and social media platforms. They can propagate false information and inflame tensions, but they can also bring people together, inspire dialogue, and give a voice to the hitherto unheard. These competing opinions may drown out the goal of harmonious cooperation and unity.

Nonetheless, hope persists despite these setbacks. We do more than take in these narratives as spectators; we also play an integral role in shaping them. We can examine, challenge, and alter these. We leave behind us data fragments that reflect our reality as we view it and as it is in this age of hyper-connectivity. A lengthy shadow is cast across the road by the rising skyscrapers of social media, whose intended purpose was to foster connection but which has devolved into a funhouse mirror of distorted realities.

These platforms have replaced the ancient arenas of Rome as the places where the most extreme ideas triumph over more moderate ones in the struggle for widespread approval. We need to hear a symphony of unity and collaboration. Unseen algorithms, also to blame for the show's other significant flaws, amplify the dissonant notes of false information and conflict.

It's like wading through a swamp of fake news as we navigate this information environment. These deceptive threads reach out from behind a facade of reliability to tangle the trusting traveler and plant seeds of uncertainty. With their deep roots and sturdy defenses, these thorns suffocate the delicate balance of sympathy and cooperation we strive to achieve.

During this anarchy, we encounter people driven by the desire for power and wealth. They use the rest of us as pawns to defend their privileged societal positions. They take advantage of social divisions to sway public opinion in their favor and foster an atmosphere of inequality and discord instead of harmony.

Our culture has much tension because of the herd mentality. When faced with such formidable forces, individuals' risk having their unique perspectives drowned out by the public. People's opinions will mirror the wishes of the powerful when they cannot think critically about the evidence presented. This has the unintended consequence of weakening the democratic mechanisms necessary for our harmonious development.

Nonetheless, there is still a glimmer of hope amidst all the confusion. Remember, as we go closer to The Transition, that every symphony begins with dissonance. We hone our hearing to distinguish between the truth's rumble and the fallout of a lie. We strive to see through the fog of social media with the bright eye of analysis and deduce what moves the social chess pieces and why. We aim to transform the crowd into a unified chorus that enhances rather than obscures the original song. This journey lies at the center of our Harmonious Evolution and is about struggle and goal.

We must also address the influence of money and power in our government. It's usual for the privileged to lose touch with the plight of the less fortunate as they rise to power, which can have a chilling effect on their ability to feel empathy and compassion. The potential for wealth to make people less empathetic and impair moral judgment adds more dissonance to our tumultuous social symphony. Furthermore, higher levels of prosperity have been linked to greater exposure to addiction difficulties, which may worsen preexisting societal differences and conflicts.

Our journey is about more than mere survival; it is also about prospering as individuals and as communities. The goal is to silence the voices of dissent and replace them with music. This is the heart of our development and progress. With each challenge we meet and conquer, we go closer to realizing our vision of a world where everyone is heard, integrity is rewarded over dishonesty, and community over competitiveness is celebrated.

The road to Harmonious Evolution begins with recognizing one's worth. It's the foundation upon which progress and transformation can occur. Confidence in one's values empowers one to make positive changes in life and the world.

It would be best if you freed yourself from the chains of other people's expectations and judgments. You, and only you, have the key to your true worth. Keep the ideas we've discussed to determine your value. You have experienced firsthand the adverse outcomes that ensue when you let other people define your worth. But I've learned something vital from countless interactions with different people: I will not let anyone make me feel less than I am.

As you embark on this mission of self-discovery, it is important to remember that you are a miraculous creation of God. Everyone in the cosmos is just as wonderfully unique as you are. Honor and revel in your individuality and quirks. You are evidence that God is faultless as a creator because His work is flawless.

If the world ever makes you doubt your worth, may you find comfort in the unchanging truth of God's Word? God's love for you is constant, and He is with you even when it seems like the world is collapsing. Take solace in the realities he spoke over you, for they are what give you worth. Follow the light of His acceptance and love as it guides you home to your authentic self.

Remember that arrogance and conceit are not the same thing as self-confidence. Realizing and appreciating your value is the key. You can maximize your abilities when you know how valuable you are. You can use them to have a positive impact on the world.

Adopting a growth mindset is essential for maintaining healthy self-worth and reaching one's greatest potential. A convincing example of the effect a growth mindset may have on one's potential to achieve great things is Michael Jordan's life.

Michael Jordan, widely regarded as the greatest basketball player of all time, experienced a significant setback early in his career. He wasn't allowed to continue playing basketball for his high school. It was a turning point that could have made him question his value and give up on his dream. Jordan, though, refused to be defined by his failure.

Instead of wallowing in his feelings of rejection, Jordan turned them into the drive to improve himself. He developed a growth mindset, believing his abilities could be honed through diligent practice. He spent many hours honing his basketball skills to be the best player he could be.

The eventual result of Jordan's hard work and faith in his abilities was fruitful. His career resulted in a remarkable one in which he became a household name worldwide and won six NBA championships. He exemplifies the importance of a "growth mindset" in action.

The belief that one's strengths and shortcomings are flexible and can be developed over time is characteristic of a growth mindset. Instead, you believe you can improve in any area, and that hard work and dedication will pay off.

Remember that the people providing you with feedback are also human and that their unfavorable worldviews, prejudices, and other factors may cause them to provide inaccurate information. Before acting on any input, it is necessary to consider where it came from and evaluate the trustworthiness and validity of the source.

Recognize that human viewpoints and biases may influence the input in a multi-perspective and small world. Attributing another person's flaws to them to make themselves feel better is a common form of projection. Consider the source and function of any feedback you receive with an open mind.

The following should be kept in mind when determining the credibility of a feedback source:

You, like everyone else, are guilty of harboring biases and making assumptions. Their judgments and opinions may color the comments they make. Try to keep an open mind and put aside your inclinations.

Examine the justifications of people who have provided feedback. Is this person genuinely interested in helping you grow, or do they have other agendas in mind? Consider your relationship with the critic and whether or not they share your aims.

Seek out different perspectives, allowing you to build a more well-rounded judgment. Get people's opinions from all walks of life and all educational backgrounds. This can aid in overcoming bias by forcing you to consider alternative viewpoints.

Assess knowledge. Consider the knowledge and credibility of the reviewer. Do they have expertise and experience in the field at hand? Do they have enough experience to provide useful suggestions? Knowing the source's expertise can help you determine how much weight to give their opinion.

In the end, rely on your common sense and intuition. You have the most intimate familiarity with your motivations, values, and capacities. Take criticism as a chance to learn and improve, but always remember that you can decide for yourself what fits your goals and values.

Let's focus on recognizing your value and following helpful instructions.

Recognizing Your Value:

Having confidence in yourself has nothing to do with arrogance or pride; rather, it stems from the realization that you, like everyone else, possess valuable qualities and have something to offer the world. Your future vision for positive change is established on this realization. It gives you the confidence to pursue ambitious goals that align with who you want to be in the future.

Plan of Attack:

First, take stock of what makes you unique. What is it that you excel at? How do you spend your free time?

The second step is to recognize the worth of these qualities. Please acknowledge that you can change the world for the better because of them.

Third, do something about it. Take advantage of your skills and abilities to propel yourself forward.

Getting Your Bearings by Having a Straight View:

Establish your goals as a first step. If you could shape the future, what would it be like? What message does it send about your priorities and sense of self-worth?

The second step is to develop specific, measurable objectives. Is there anything you can do to turn your dream into a reality?

The third stage entails communicating your vision to others. Share your dreams and ambitions with the world and ask for help realizing them.

You can travel the path of Harmonious Evolution with confidence and bravery if you know your worth and accept your vision. Remember that while the ocean may be large and the journey may be difficult, you can sail your ship toward a future of growth, fulfillment, and sound change with a clear vision and a strong feeling of your value.

Strengthening One's Confidence:

Belief in yourself is the steady rhythmic pulse that drives you ahead on the path to Harmonious Evolution. Self-confidence may get you far in life. It fortifies your determination, increases your fortitude, and magnifies your power to effect transformation. It is a constant reminder that you can steer your route, even in unfamiliar territory.

Take Oprah Winfrey, who overcame extreme disadvantages to become a media mogul and a force for positive social change. Her unshakeable confidence was the driving force behind her rise to media mogul and global powerhouse status.

Building confidence is the first step. Think back on the things you've accomplished, the qualities you possess, and the challenges you've already overcome.

Second, try to argue with your negative thoughts. In the face of doubt, remind yourself of your strengths and the progress you've already made.

Third, fill your environment with upbeat people. Spend time with people and do things that boost your confidence and motivate you to keep going.

Accepting Change:

Value self-awareness and have a clear vision but remember to be adaptable. Life's waves are choppy, and the winds of change can instantly throw you off course. The ability to pivot means you may adjust your sails to take advantage of favorable breezes and transform difficulties into gains. It's an admission that, though your destination is fixed, how you get there can change.

Take Apple Inc.'s history as a real-world illustration. Apple's first market concentration was on desktop and laptop computers. However, Apple saw the changing tides in technology and steered into uncharted waters, such as the music industry (iPod), the telecommunications industry (iPhone), and the wearable technology market (Apple Watch). Apple's continued success and influence on the technology industry can be attributed to the company's adaptability.

First, commit to adopting a "growth mindset." Reframe difficulties as educational and developmental challenges.

Second, take criticism seriously. Learn from the experiences of others and adjust your course accordingly.

Third, evaluate your progress along the way frequently. Is the road you're on taking you closer to realizing your goals? If that's the case, what changes can you make?

Collaboration:

Please don't go through life without company; we were made for conversation. There is no such thing as a solo trip. Our activities have consequences beyond ourselves and impact the world around us. The key to successfully implementing change and encouraging peaceful progress is valuing people and forming collaborations.

The first thing to do is try to get people to work together. Find people, groups, or businesses whose ideals are similar to yours and see if you can work together.

Second, work to increase trust and communication among team members. Appreciate the differences in expertise and point of view between you and the other person.

Third, rejoice in your group's achievements. Recognize the successes accomplished together and give credit where credit is due.

Encourage Continuous Education:

The path to Harmonious Evolution is fueled by continuous education. It's about learning new things and growing wiser as you go through life. Adapting to new circumstances, taking on new tasks, and making the most of unforeseen possibilities result from a commitment to lifelong learning and improvement.

Take Albert Einstein, the great physicist, as a real-world example. He was always curious about new things and eager to expand his knowledge. His dogged curiosity yielded notions that shook our foundational beliefs about the cosmos.

First, encourage a sense of wonder. Inquire and look for clarification. You can use this to further your education.

The second step is to welcome a range of educational experiences. The classrooms of life include books, classes, conversations, and experiences.

Third, consider how you can use what you've learned. Think about what you've learned and how it can regularly help you on your path to Harmonious Evolution.

Additional Step-by-Step Action Plan for Embracing Self-Worth and Overcoming Negative Stories:

1. Examine the Stories: Take time to reflect on the stories you tell yourself that make you feel less than you are. Question the social signals and narratives influencing your perception of beauty and value. Recognize that these stories are often constructed and propagated by those with ulterior motives.

- a. **Journaling:** Write down the negative stories you often tell yourself and the external influences contributing to them. Reflect on how these narratives have affected your self-worth.
- b. **Critical Analysis:** Challenge the validity of these stories and consider alternative perspectives that empower and uplift you.
- c. **Seek Knowledge:** Educate yourself about societal standards of beauty and value to understand their origins and how they can be distorted.

2. Affirm Your Worth: Counter critical thoughts with positive affirmations that affirm your inherent value and uniqueness. Cultivate a positive mindset and reinforce your self-worth through daily affirmations and vision boards.

- a. **Affirmation Practice:** Create a list of positive affirmations that reflect your value and worth. Repeat them daily and internalize them as truths about yourself.
- b. **Vision Board:** Create a visual representation of your aspirations and positive qualities. Include images, quotes, and words that inspire and remind you of your worth.
- c. **Self-Reflection:** Regularly reflect on your positive attributes, achievements, and impact on others. Celebrate your strengths and acknowledge your growth.

3. Develop Yourself from Within: Shift your focus from seeking approval from others to self-improvement and personal growth. Embrace becoming the best version of yourself by nurturing your talents, skills, and passions.

   a. **Continuous Learning:** Cultivate a love for learning and seek opportunities to expand your knowledge and skills. Engage in courses, workshops, or self-study to enhance your personal development.
   b. **Cultivate Positivity:** Surround yourself with positive influences, whether it's through books, podcasts, or online communities. Seek inspiration from those who have overcome challenges and cultivated a strong sense of self-worth.

4. Create a Supportive Environment: Surround yourself with people who accept and value you for who you are. Seek individuals and communities promoting self-love, acceptance, and personal growth.

   a. **Choose Your Circle:** Assess the people in your life and identify those who uplift and support you. Limit or eliminate interactions with individuals who consistently undermine your self-worth.
   b. **Join Supportive Communities:** Find clubs, organizations, or support groups that align with your values and provide a nurturing environment. Engage in activities that promote self-acceptance and appreciation of others.
   c. **Foster Relationships:** Cultivate meaningful relationships with people who genuinely care about your well-being and encourage your personal growth. Surround yourself with individuals who see your value and inspire you to embrace it.

5. Prioritize Self-Care: Dedicate time to nurturing your mental, physical, and spiritual well-being. Engage in self-care practices that promote self-love, mindfulness, and overall wellness.

a. **Physical Health:** Engage in regular exercise or physical activities that bring you joy and boost your self-confidence. Prioritize nutritious meals and quality sleep to support your overall well-being.
b. **Mental Health:** Practice mindfulness, meditation, or journaling to cultivate self-awareness and manage stress. Seek professional help if needed to address any underlying mental health concerns.
c. **Spiritual Nourishment:** Connect with your spirituality through meditation, prayer, or time in nature. Engage in activities that bring you a sense of inner peace and fulfillment.

Remember that accepting others has nothing to do with your value or attractiveness. You should be loved and accepted for who you are and what you provide to the world. Recognize your worth and acknowledge that you are more than the sum of the world's opinions and expectations. Restoring your sense of value, honoring your individuality, and shining your inner beauty on the world are all steps toward Harmonious Evolution, which aims to foster peace and acceptance.

Now that we've reached the end of this section, it's important to think back on the monumental path we've traveled so far. The Transition is a watershed moment, the point at which we enter the world of dynamic transition. It's a chance to start fresh and reject negative habits and worldviews in favor of those that will lead to a happier, healthier you. We ride the waves of change with compassion and foresight, hoping to bring about a more peaceful development in ourselves and the world around us.

This chapter discusses the value of a growth mindset and the significance of knowing our own worth. We have explored the nuances of worldviews and their potential effects on our sense of worth as individuals. We covered how critical it is to assess the credibility of input before acting on it. And through it all, we've learned that we have what it takes to ignore the naysayers and forge our path to success and happiness.

The examples of people who have battled against the odds and prevailed have fueled our quest for peaceful development. The extraordinary rise of Michael Jordan, who was cut from his high school basketball team before becoming the greatest NBA player in history, is a prime example. His experience teaches us that we are more than our failures and detractors. Instead, they should be seen as challenges that can be overcome with perseverance and faith in one's abilities.

Along our path through The Transition, we must also recognize that we are susceptible to the same prejudices and influences as everyone else. If we let them, outside influences can alter how we see the world and feel about ourselves. But with the wisdom and insight obtained on this journey of metamorphosis, we can combat those forces and establish our worth.

Always maintain that our value is independent of the transient views of others. We are all unique in our ways, wonderfully made, and endowed with the power to make a difference in the world. We can write stories and reframe our value according to our unique skills, experiences, and accomplishments.

Let us take the lessons of this chapter with us into the next. Recognize your value and foster a growth attitude to drive your pursuit of excellence. Be aware of the potential biases and influences that can shape feedback, and exercise discernment in selecting and incorporating only that which resonates with your true self. Trust in your good sense and instincts, and know you can successfully make it through this time of change.

The following chapter will cover "embracing personal growth and development" in the context of Transformative Growth. We will look into how self-reflection can help us see, free us from the constraints of the past, and usher in a period of rapid personal development. So, my reader, relax, think, and get ready for an epic adventure.

Finally, remember that you are a unique person with the power to improve your life and the world at large. You will find your true potential and feel the transformational power of harmonious evolution throughout the Transition. Therefore, welcome it with open arms.

Your journey thus far reflects your strength, resilience, and unyielding commitment to personal growth and positive transformation, and it is with appreciation and eagerness that we encourage you to keep going toward a more balanced, satisfying life.

Chapter 12

Transformative Growth - The Peak (Embracing personal growth and Development)

At the summit of The Peak, there is a distinct energy in the air that can be felt, almost as if the essence of change and personal development remains in every breath. It is a holy place, a lookout point that provides a 360-degree panorama of the path you have traveled up to this point on your journey. You can't help but be impressed with your accomplishments and the person you've grown into when you reach the mountain's summit.

In this pause for reflection, you allow yourself to reflect on the successes that have dotted your journey. Each victory demonstrates your resiliency and unyielding drive to break free from the confines that the past has placed on you. You are astounded by the challenges you have overcome, the obstacles you have broken through, and the boundaries you have disregarded. The Peak is the stage upon which you have earned the right to reflect on how far you have come and the person you have developed into.

However, it's not just the victories that capture your interest; there are other things. Your eyes are drawn to the obstacles thrown along the path of your rise, much like stones. You will never forget the failures, the detours, and the moments of doubt because they have permanently imprinted themselves into your memory. However, now that you are standing at The Peak, you see that the challenges you faced were not roadblocks but stepping stones. They served as the furnaces that shaped your personality, honed your resolve, and strengthened your resiliency. Every misstep and setback have the potential to become a priceless education, a wellspring of insight that will serve as a compass for you as you continue on your path to self-improvement.

The Peak is not the finish line but the beginning of something new and exciting. It encourages you to keep ascending and discover the countless opportunities waiting for you beyond the horizon. From this vantage position, you will have a more distinct view of the route that lies in front of you, which will be enlightened by the brilliant light of God's Word. It is a light that guides your feet, infusing you with the confidence and knowledge that you are never alone on this road of self-transformation.

You take a few deep breaths and let the enormity of The Peak wash over you. As you do this, tremendous thankfulness arises within your heart. Recognition and gratitude for the struggles that have helped you become more robust, the successes that have encouraged you, and the unyielding faith that has carried you through it all. The Peak demonstrates the transformative potential of personal and spiritual development; it is a gentle nudge toward new horizons and a call to accept the totality of who you were created to be.

You have attained this higher state of consciousness. As a result, you are aware that the worldviews presented by modern technology, social media sites, and movies are not absolute facts but rather interpretations filtered through the storyteller's lens. They might try to mold your perceptions, establish your value, or box you within predetermined parameters. On the other hand, you have overcome these restrictions and are now unrestricted to enjoy The Peak's natural beauty and majesty.

The Light Path illuminated your path, offering clarity among the din and mayhem of the world around you. It has taught you how to differentiate the stories others tell from the reality deep within your being and has directed you to do so successfully. You have realized that your road to The Peak is an individual one, formed by the experiences, beliefs, and values specific to you. You are a living example of the strength of remaining unwavering in your commitment to who you are as an individual, unmoved by the ever-shifting currents of the demands placed upon us by society.

Although new technologies, social media platforms, and movies might offer valuable insights and viewpoints, you have learned to approach them with a discernment that befits someone with your experience. You know these things are not infallible truth sources but instruments that can be used for beneficial or harmful purposes, depending on how they are used. With this knowledge, you can navigate the wide world of media and entertainment, selecting storylines congruent with your beliefs, resonate with your inner reality, and inspire you to be your best self.

Your ascent to The Peak has not only helped you become more self-aware, but it has also helped you fall in love with yourself. You have developed an unwavering faith in your worth, and you are aware that your value is not contingent on other people's opinions or the narratives presented by the world. On the other hand, you have taken ownership of the ability to determine your own value, honoring your singularity and valuing the splendor that is already present within you.

While standing at The Peak, you can't help but reflect on the immense possibility ahead of you and the breadth of your potential. You have shown that you are willing to break free from the confines of conventional standards and expectations and have welcomed the freedom to do so. You have emerged as a guiding light for others, illuminating the path to genuine emancipation by illustrating how it may be attained from within through an unbreakable connection to one's inner truth and the unconditional love and acceptance of the Divine.

When you reach The Peak, you shine with the brilliance of genuineness and fortitude. You are a living witness to the transformational power of accepting your authentic self and challenging the perspectives of the world. Thank you for sharing your story. You motivate others to go out on their path of introspection and develop their personal qualities with each step you take along the Light Path. Those individuals who dare to liberate themselves from the bounds of cultural conditioning are the ones who will find that the world is brimming with unfathomable opportunities that are just waiting to be discovered and grasped. Your presence is a constant reminder of this truth.

As you continue your ascent from The Peak, you carry the understanding and power you gained from traveling along this transforming path. You know that the Light Path does not go to a specific location but is a continuous personal development and advancement process. You take on each new obstacle as an opportunity to learn more about yourself, grow, and relish both prospects. **You are:**

- A change agent
- A catalyst for harmonic progress.
- This is a living example of the power of accepting personal growth and development.
- You are a monument to the importance of these things.

You are about to begin the next stage of your trip, and the Light Path will serve as your guide. You are prepared to confront new horizons, triumph over new challenges, and continue shattering barriers. The Peak is the first step to even higher heights, just the starting point. As you continue your journey, remember what you've picked up, how you've grown, and your limitless potential. Embrace the transforming power of your path and keep shining your light brilliantly, igniting the world with your authenticity, love, and unrelenting commitment to breaking free from the world's views. Embrace the transformative power of your journey and continue to shine your light brightly.

Aisha's Story:

A young woman named Aisha Patel lived in the vibrant city of Mumbai, nestled amidst the bustling streets and colorful bazaars. Aisha, with her deep roots in Indian culture and her unwavering spirit, was on a remarkable journey of self-discovery and personal growth. Her family had immigrated to Mumbai generations ago, seeking a better life and new opportunities.

She grew up surrounded by the sights, sounds, and flavors that infused her daily life, shaping her perspective and fueling her curiosity about the world. Mumbai was a city of contrasts, where ancient traditions coexisted with modernity, and Aisha navigated the intricacies of this dynamic landscape.

As Aisha entered her teenage years, she met a friend named Susan, who had recently moved to Mumbai from Florida. Susan was drawn to the city's vibrant energy and was eager to immerse herself in Mumbai's culture and traditions. The two young women quickly became inseparable, their friendship blossoming amidst the chaos and beauty of the city.

Susan's perspective as an outsider provided a fresh lens through which Aisha could view her own culture and heritage. Together, they embarked on countless adventures, exploring the hidden gems of Mumbai and venturing beyond the beaten path. They wandered through the labyrinthine lanes of the old city, marveling at the ancient architecture and indulging in mouthwatering street food. They attended colorful festivals, their senses awakened by the melodies of traditional music and the vibrant hues of saris adorning the locals.

As the years passed, Aisha and Susan became more than just friends—they became each other's confidantes, sources of inspiration, and pillars of support. They navigated the challenges of adolescence together, weathering storms of self-doubt and societal expectations. They learned to embrace their individuality through their bond, celebrating their unique strengths and quirks.

After completing high school, Susan returned to her hometown of Florida to pursue higher education. Aisha bid her farewell with a heavy heart, knowing that their paths would diverge for a while. However, their connection remained steadfast, as they promised to keep each other's dreams alive, no matter the distance.

While in Mumbai, Aisha witnessed marginalized communities' immense challenges, particularly in accessing quality education. Inspired by her experiences and driven by her desire to make a difference, she became involved in various social initiatives. She volunteered at local NGOs, helping to provide education and support to underprivileged children. Through these experiences, Aisha discovered the transformative power of education and its ability to empower individuals and uplift communities.

As Aisha's passion for social justice grew, she decided to pursue a degree in social work. With Susan's unwavering support from across the ocean, Aisha applied to universities in Florida, hoping to continue her journey of personal growth and positive impact globally. After months of anticipation, she received an acceptance letter from a prestigious university in Florida, and her dream of studying abroad became a reality.

Aisha's transition to life in Florida was both exciting and challenging. She navigated a new cultural landscape, adapting to customs and social norms. However, her Indian heritage served as a strong foundation, providing her with a sense of identity and grounding her in times of uncertainty. Aisha's openness to new experiences and her ability to embrace diversity allowed her to forge meaningful connections with people from all walks of life.

In Florida, Aisha discovered a vibrant Indian community that welcomed her with open arms. She found comfort in their shared traditions, celebrations, and the flavors of home that reminded her of Mumbai.

Through her involvement in cultural organizations and events, Aisha became a bridge between cultures, fostering understanding and appreciation for the beauty of diversity.

As Aisha continued her studies, she became increasingly aware of the world's views and their impact on individuals' self-worth. She witnessed the pervasive influence of media, social expectations, and societal pressures on shaping people's identities and limiting their potential. Aisha was determined to challenge these views for herself and others trapped within societal norms.

Through her tireless efforts, Aisha became a role model for young women of Indian descent, showing them they could navigate cultural identity complexities while pursuing their dreams and creating positive change. She shattered stereotypes, defied expectations, and opened doors for others to follow in her footsteps.

As Aisha stood at the forefront of her movement, she recognized the power of collective action. She founded an organization empowering young women from marginalized communities, providing them mentorship, educational opportunities, and a platform to amplify their voices. Aisha's organization catalyzed change, fostering a sense of sisterhood and unity among these young women, who were now determined to break barriers and defy the world's views.

Aisha's journey had come full circle, from the streets of Mumbai to the shores of Florida. She embraced her Indian heritage, nurtured her personal growth, and used her voice to challenge the world's views. Through her unwavering spirit, resilience, and belief in unity, Aisha became a beacon of hope, inspiring others to unleash their true potential and create a world that celebrated diversity and compassion.

As the sun set on Aisha's extraordinary journey, she knew her story was far from over. She continued to learn, grow, and evolve with each new day. She remained committed to uplifting others, embracing her roots, and challenging the world's views. As Aisha's journey unfolded, it became apparent that there was a profound connection between her personal growth and the concept of the Light Path. Although the

Light Path had not yet been defined in her story, her journey shared striking similarities with the transformative path illuminated by its guiding light.

As we understand it today, the Light Path represents a journey of self-discovery, personal growth, and spiritual awakening. It is a path that leads individuals toward their true selves, guiding them through the complexities of life and empowering them to embrace their unique identities.

Aisha's journey echoed the essence of the Light Path. She embarked on a quest to uncover her true self and challenge the world's views that sought to confine her. She encountered obstacles, setbacks, and moments of doubt along the way. However, her unwavering determination and resilience kept her moving forward, much like the guiding light of the Light Path.

Just as the Light Path offers clarity amidst the chaos, Aisha found solace in her Indian heritage, grounding her in times of uncertainty and providing a sense of identity. Her connection to her roots was a guiding force, illuminating her path and allowing her to navigate the challenges she encountered.

In her pursuit of building relationships, Aisha applied the principles of empathy and understanding she had developed along the way, similar to the Light Path. She recognized that every individual she encountered had their own unique story, perspectives, and struggles. Aisha approached her interactions with an open heart and mind, seeking to connect on a deeper level and foster genuine connections.

One area where Aisha actively sought to build relationships was in her professional life. As she transitioned from Mumbai to Florida, she immersed herself in the local community, attending networking events and seeking opportunities to collaborate with like-minded professionals. Aisha understood that building a strong professional network opened doors for growth and career opportunities and provided a support system for individuals who shared similar goals and aspirations.

In her personal life, Aisha cultivated deep connections with her family and friends. She recognized the importance of nurturing these relationships and investing time and effort into creating meaningful bonds. Aisha prioritized spending quality time with her loved ones, engaging in activities that brought them closer together, and creating lasting memories. She understood that the richness of life came from the shared experiences and the love and support of those closest to her.

But Aisha didn't stop there. She also sought to build relationships beyond her immediate circles, reaching out to individuals from diverse backgrounds and cultures. She actively participated in community events, volunteering her time and skills to make a positive impact. Aisha recognized that embracing diversity and connecting with people from different walks of life could broaden her perspectives, challenge her assumptions, and contribute to a more inclusive and harmonious world.

Finally, Aisha's relationship with God was central to her journey. Her connection to the divine provided guidance, strength, and comfort as she navigated the ups and downs of her transformative path. Through prayer, reflection, and spiritual practices, Aisha deepened her faith and found solace in knowing she was never alone. Her relationship with God provided a sense of purpose and direction, anchoring her as she broke free from the unseen chains of societal worldviews.

As Aisha broke free from the unseen chains of societal worldviews, she embraced a newfound freedom and authenticity. She liberated herself and her loved ones from the confines of generational cruises, creating a new narrative rooted in self-empowerment, love, and acceptance. Aisha's courageous pursuit of personal growth and the transformation of her relationships catalyzed change, inspiring others to question societal norms and embark on their journeys of liberation.

Ultimately, Aisha's journey was not just about her liberation but about the liberation of future generations. By breaking the unseen chains of societal worldviews and embracing her true self, she forged a new path for her family, friends, and all those who would come after her. Aisha's story is a powerful reminder that we can challenge societal norms, build authentic relationships, and create a world that celebrates and uplifts every individual's inherent beauty and worth.

Now that we finish exploring Aisha's story picture this: You're standing on the edge of a breathtaking mountain peak, the air crisp and invigorating as it fills your lungs. The sun's golden rays illuminate the surrounding landscape, revealing a vista that stretches as far as the eye can see. Your heart pounds with anticipation, knowing that these peak promises something extraordinary that will transform your life in ways you never thought possible.

But here's the twist: This isn't just any mountain peak. This is the Peak, an acronym representing a groundbreaking program that will take you on a journey like no other. Each letter of the word "Peak" represents a step, a milestone, an experience that will push you beyond your limits and unlock your hidden potential.

P - Puzzle Your Perspectives
E - Explore Experiential Realms
A - Awaken Inner Alchemy
K - Kindle your Inner Drive

Are you ready to embark on this extraordinary adventure? The Peak program is not for the faint of heart. It's for those who dare to dream big, yearn for more from life, and are willing to push themselves beyond their comfort zones. It's a journey that will test your resilience, ignite your passions, and unleash the greatness that lies dormant within you.

During the Prepare for the Climb phase, you'll equip yourself with the tools and mindset necessary to conquer any obstacle that stands in your way. You'll learn to harness the power of your thoughts, develop unwavering self-belief, and cultivate a strong foundation for your journey ahead.

As you Embrace the Unknown, you'll embrace the beauty of uncertainty and dive headfirst into uncharted territories. You'll learn to embrace failure as a stepping stone to success, to dance with discomfort, and to see challenges as opportunities for growth.

Then comes the moment you've been waiting for – Ascend to New Heights. Here, you'll push yourself to the limits, breaking through self-imposed barriers and conquering the seemingly insurmountable. You'll discover new strengths, unleash hidden talents, and bask in the glory of your achievements as you climb higher and higher toward your peak.

So, are you ready to take the first step towards your Peak? Are you ready to embrace the extraordinary, unlock your true potential, and stand proudly on the summit of your greatness? The Peak program awaits you. Get ready to embark on the adventure of a lifetime.

The Peak program:

Step 1: P - Puzzle Your Perspectives

Paradoxical Thinking: Embrace paradoxes and contradictions to challenge your usual ways of thinking. Engage in mind-bending exercises that force you to question assumptions and see situations from multiple angles. Break free from mental rigidity and expand your problem-solving capabilities.

For example:
- Recognize the limitations of rigid worldviews on considering alternative perspectives.

How?
- Self-reflect and question biases.
- Seek diverse input and listen attentively.
- Challenge confirmation bias and seek diverse information.
- Embrace paradoxes and contradictions to challenge narrow thinking patterns.

How?
- Embrace intellectual discomfort.
- Engage in critical thinking and question assumptions.
- Cultivate open-mindedness and receptiveness.
- Engage in mind-bending exercises to break free from fixed beliefs and explore new possibilities.

How?
- Experiment with new experiences.
- Seek diverse sources of information.
- Practice cognitive flexibility and creative problem-solving.

Perspective Journeys: Take part in immersive experiences that expose you to unfamiliar perspectives. Engage with diverse communities, cultures, or environments that stretch your worldview. Engage in role-playing activities that require you to embody different personas and see the world through their eyes.

For example:
- Acknowledge biases created by worldviews and hindrances to understanding diverse perspectives.

How?
- Practice active listening and seek to understand different viewpoints.
- Engage in meaningful conversations with individuals from diverse backgrounds.
- Challenge assumptions and preconceived notions about others.
- Seek immersive experiences exposed to unfamiliar cultures, communities, and environments.

How?
- Engage in travel or cultural exchange programs that allow you to immerse yourself in unfamiliar cultures, communities, and environments.
- Seek out local events, festivals, or gatherings where you can interact with people from different backgrounds.
- Embrace the discomfort of encountering different worldviews to expand empathy and tolerance.

How?
- Approach conversations and interactions with individuals who hold different worldviews with an open mind and genuine curiosity.
- Engage in empathy-building exercises, such as role-playing or storytelling, to put yourself in the shoes of someone with a different worldview and truly understand their experiences and beliefs.

Playful Synchronicity: Cultivate a playful mindset and seek synchronicities in everyday life. Notice patterns and coincidences that may hold hidden messages or insights. Engage in creative activities that spark serendipity and encourage unconventional connections.

For example:
Recognize how rigid worldviews can blind us to subtle connections and patterns.

How?
- Seek opportunities to participate in intercultural dialogues, workshops, or events that foster understanding and appreciation for different perspectives.
- Cultivate a playful mindset to see beyond our narrow worldview and embrace synchronicities.

How?
- Explore new hobbies, interests, or fields of knowledge outside your comfort zone, broadening your horizons and expanding your understanding of the world.
- Notice hidden messages or insights and engage in creative activities to encourage unconventional connections.

How?
- Pay attention to the messages being delivered and discern the true agenda.

Step 2: E - Explore Experiential Realms

Embodied Embarkation: Immerse yourself in physical experiences challenging your body and senses. Engage in adventure sports, dance, martial arts, or kinesthetic activities that push your boundaries and enhance body awareness.

For example:
- Recognize the limitations of worldviews on physical experiences and body engagement.

How?
- Question and challenge the assumptions and limitations imposed by our beliefs about what our bodies can or cannot do.
- Open ourselves to new possibilities by exploring various physical activities and pushing beyond our comfort zones.
- Challenge fixed beliefs hindering exploration of new physical activities.

How?
- Embrace the process of learning and growth as we challenge and overcome the self-imposed restrictions of our beliefs.

- Seek opportunities to expand our physical horizons and engage in activities that challenge our preconceived notions of what our bodies are capable of.
- Embrace adventure sports, dance, or martial arts to break free from worldview constraints.

Eclectic Encounters: Seek diverse encounters with people, places, and ideas. Engage in conversations with individuals from different backgrounds and disciplines. Explore unconventional spaces and subcultures that defy societal norms. Embrace the richness of serendipitous encounters and unexpected connections.

For example:

- Visit art galleries, museums, or exhibitions showcasing a variety of artistic expressions and cultural artifacts.
- Travel to destinations off the beaten path, seeking encounters with local communities and immersing yourself in their customs and traditions.

Experimental Expeditions: Design and undertake experimental journeys that push the boundaries of your comfort zone. Plan trips to unexplored destinations, engage in social experiments or embark on creative endeavors with no predefined outcomes. Embrace the uncertainty and learn from the unexpected.

For example:

- Participate in a social experiment or volunteer program that exposes you to different communities and societal issues, allowing you to learn and contribute uniquely.
- Engage in creative endeavors with no predefined outcomes, such as improvisational theater, abstract painting, or experimental writing, allowing your creativity to flow freely and explore new possibilities.

Step 3: A - Awaken Inner Alchemy

Artistic Alchemy: Tap into your creative potential through various artistic expressions. Engage in painting, writing, music, or any other artistic form that allows you to explore your emotions and channel your innermost thoughts. Embrace the transformative power of creativity.

For example:
- Create a personal art sanctuary in your home to immerse yourself in a creative environment. Surround yourself with inspiring artworks, books, and materials that fuel your imagination and invite you to explore new artistic expressions.
- Incorporate artistic practices into your daily life, such as practicing mindful doodling or engaging in spontaneous writing exercises. Use these creative outlets to process your emotions, release stress, and tap into the transformative power of art as a form of self-expression.

Authentic Connections: Foster deep and meaningful connections with others based on authenticity and vulnerability. Engage in activities that promote trust-building, active listening, and empathy. Create spaces for open dialogue and shared experiences that foster profound connections.

For example:
- **Storytelling Circles:** Gather a group of friends or acquaintances and create a safe and supportive space for storytelling. Encourage each person to share a personal story or experience that has shaped their lives. Through active listening and genuine curiosity, foster an environment where vulnerability is embraced, and authentic connections are formed.
- **Collaboration Projects:** Initiate collaborative projects that require individuals from diverse backgrounds to work together

towards a common goal. By fostering teamwork, shared responsibility, and open communication, these projects create opportunities for authentic connections to flourish and meaningful relationships to develop. If you find that church events, small groups, or serving foster this type of collaboration of people with different backgrounds and races.

Step 4: K – Kindle your Inner Drive

Clarify Your Passions: Reflect on your passions and interests. Identify what truly ignites your inner fire and brings you a sense of purpose and fulfillment. Focus your time and energy on pursuing activities aligned with your passions.

For example:
- Make a list of activities or hobbies that you enjoy and that make you feel alive and fulfilled.
- Reflect on moments when you felt a deep sense of joy, excitement, or purpose.
- Consider the values and principles important to you and how they connect to your passions.
- Experiment with new activist activity experiences to uncover new passions and interests.

Set Purposeful Intentions: Define clear intentions and goals that align with your passions. Create a roadmap for achieving them and take consistent action towards their realization.

For example:
- Break down your intentions into actionable goals that are measurable and attainable.
- Create a roadmap or plan that outlines the steps you need to take to achieve your goals.

- Prioritize your goals based on their importance and relevance to your passions.
- Take consistent action towards your goals, setting aside dedicated time and effort to work on them.
- Monitor your progress regularly and make adjustments to your plan as needed.
- Stay committed and focused on your intentions, maintaining a sense of purpose and drive.
- Seek support and accountability from others who can help you stay on track and provide guidance.
- Celebrate milestones and achievements along the way to stay motivated and inspired.

Cultivate Self-Motivation: Develop strategies to maintain and fuel your inner fire. Surround yourself with positive influences, practice self-care, and celebrate small wins. Stay motivated by reminding yourself of your purpose and the impact you want to make in the world.

For example:
- Surround yourself with positive influences and individuals who inspire and uplift you.
- Practice self-care to ensure your physical, mental, and emotional well-being.
- Set aside tie for activities that recharge and energize you, such as exercise, meditation, or hobbies.
- Develop a positive mindset by focusing on gratitude, affirmations, and self-belief.
- Seek support and accountability from mentors, coaches, or like-minded individuals who can encourage and motivate you.

Remember, this creative action plan is designed to spark unconventional thinking and push the boundaries of personal growth. Embrace the spirit of adventure and tailor these steps to suit your unique preferences and aspirations. Enjoy the journey as you explore uncharted territories and unlock new dimensions of personal transformation.

My Personal Story:

As I embarked on my journey to the summit of the Peak, I could never have anticipated the profound transformations that awaited me. Each step brought me closer to breaking free from my fixed mindset and challenging the limiting beliefs that had held me back. One of the most compelling and memorable experiences on this path of growth was the expansion of my physical horizons.

In the past, I had viewed certain activities through the lens of societal expectations and preconceived notions. I believed that specific adventures were reserved for certain races, and I had internalized the fear-driven mindset that discouraged people like me from venturing outside their comfort zones. Skiing, snowboarding, hiking, whitewater rafting, and other outdoor pursuits seemed distant and unattainable as if they were only meant for others.

However, destiny had a different plan for me. During this transformative journey, I encountered a remarkable Vietnamese woman who would become my wife. Her vibrant spirit and zest for life opened my eyes to the beauty and excitement that awaited me beyond the boundaries of my fixed mindset. She challenged me to break free from the confines of my comfort zone and experience the thrill of exploring the great outdoors.

I jokingly referred to myself as a "city boy" who preferred the safety of indoor activities like basketball. But my wife saw the untapped potential within me and encouraged me to step outside of my self-imposed limitations. With her unwavering support and belief in me, I embarked on my first adventure, skiing and snowboarding.

As I stood on the snow-covered slopes, fear gripped me. Thoughts of potential injuries and failure flooded my mind. But I was determined to push through. I fell multiple times; each reminded me of the internal barriers I needed to overcome. Despite the challenges, I persevered, refusing to let fear dictate my actions. And in that process, I discovered a newfound sense of accomplishment and a deep connection with nature. The snow-capped mountains became a canvas for self-expression, and the exhilaration of gliding down the slopes filled me with a sense of freedom I had never known before.

Buoyed by the success of my first endeavor, I eagerly embraced the following challenge: white water rafting. This time, my mind conjured up images of being thrown from the raft and the possibility of drowning. The absence of people who looked like me further fueled my apprehension. But as we navigated the rushing rapids, adrenaline coursed through my veins. I paddled with determination, feeling the cold-water splash against my face. In those moments, I realized fear had no power over me when I embraced the unknown. The beauty of the surroundings, the unity within the raft, and the triumph of conquering each rapid filled me with peace and exhilaration.

Since then, I have embarked on countless adventures with my wife, each expanding my horizons and defying the limitations of my worldview. Parasailing, rappelling down a 300-foot mountain, spelunking in an underground water cave—each experience has etched indelible memories into the fabric of my being. Through these physical challenges, I discovered the depths of my resilience and witnessed the transformational power of stepping beyond our perceived limitations.

What I have learned on this journey is that personal growth extends beyond the confines of our minds. It encompasses our physical selves as well. As I pushed myself to embrace these new experiences, I encountered individuals from diverse backgrounds and races who shared the same exhilaration and joy. Their presence reminded me that we are all united in our pursuit of a complete life, unencumbered by regret or self-imposed restrictions.

The journey to the Peak has taught me that our transformation is not solely confined to our thoughts and beliefs—it extends to every facet of our being. It has shown me that our physical experiences are intertwined with our mental and emotional growth, offering us the opportunity to break free from the constraints of societal expectations and embrace the fullness of life.

As I stand here, reflecting on the incredible journey that has led me to this point, I am filled with profound gratitude. The physical adventures shared with my wife and other like-minded individuals have expanded my perspective and contributed to the legacy I hope to leave behind. The experiences I have embraced and the people I have met have shaped me into a more open-minded, compassionate, and resilient individual.

So, as you embark on your transformative journey, remember that personal growth encompasses exploring your inner landscape and the liberation of your physical self. Embrace the opportunities beyond your comfort zone, for you will discover your true potential in those moments of discomfort and exhilaration. Allow yourself to be guided by the wisdom of the Peak, where each step, each experience, and each challenge catalyze your transformation.

May you break free from the shackles of your fixed mindset and venture into the unknown with an open heart and an unwavering belief in your abilities. Embrace the physical adventures that beckon you, for they hold the power to unlock hidden reserves of strength, resilience, and joy. And in doing so, may you not only transform yourself but inspire others to embark on their extraordinary journeys.

Remember, the Peak is not simply a destination but a state of being. It is the culmination of our efforts, willingness to push beyond our limits, and commitment to live a life of purpose and fulfillment. As you ascend, let the spirit of the Peak guide your every step, propelling you toward the summit of your most authentic self. Embrace the physical and spiritual growth that awaits you, for within it lies the power to leave an indelible mark on the world—a legacy that will inspire future generations.

Closing Reflections:

As we take in the view from the top of the Peak, we are overcome with a tremendous sense of amazement and thankfulness for the incredible trek we have just completed. The struggles we overcame, the viewpoints we questioned, the experiences we welcomed, and the passion we stoked within ourselves have all contributed to the formation of the people we are now. As we take a moment to sit and contemplate the transformational power of the Peak, we are amazed by the tremendous amount of personal development and progress that has occurred along the journey.

The expedition to the Peak has been a transformative trip for us, leading us through the innermost recesses of our beings and illuminating the latent potential that lies inside us. The stages of P for Puzzle Your Perspectives, E for Explore Experiential Realms, A for Awaken Inner Alchemy, and K for Kindle Your Inner Drive have advanced us to self-realization and personal development. Let us now go deeper into the significant impact each step has had on our lives and the lasting changes they have brought about as a result of their presence.

We began the process of puzzling out your perspectives with the first phase, which was a journey of profound introspection and self-reflection. We were forced to acknowledge the shortcomings of our preconceived notions of the world to engage in a bold investigation of contrasting points of view. We broke free from the limits of limited thought patterns and broadened our cognitive boundaries by welcoming paradoxes and contradictions into our thinking. We were able to break free from the shackles of our preconceived notions and enter the realm of new possibilities by engaging in mentally taxing activities and being presented with obstacles that prompted deep contemplation. Puzzle Your Perspectives instilled in us the priceless ability of critical thinking and furnished us with the resources necessary to manage the difficulties of everyday life with an open and adaptable mind.

The second part of the process was titled "Explore Experiential Realms," it encouraged us to go outside of our comfort zones and become fully immersed in the many cultures, communities, and ideas. We went out of our way to have experiences that would expand the bounds of our knowledge and shake up the ideas that we had formed in our heads. Our perspectives were enlarged, and we developed a great sense of empathy and understanding from conversing with people whose histories and fields of study were very different. We were able to break free from the confines of society's standards and find the joys of fortuitous connections and surprising insights due to our exploration of unorthodox venues and subcultures. Exploring Experiential Realms opened our eyes to the interwoven nature of humanity and sparked a profound admiration for the depth of our shared human experience.

The third stage of the Peak, titled "Awaken Inner Alchemy," enabled us to connect with the source of our latent creative ability. We immersed ourselves in artistic expressions, letting our feelings run wild through painting, poetry, music, or any other creative effort that struck our fancy. Within this holy place's confines, we could excavate the depths of our most private thoughts and tap into the transformational power of our creative abilities. Through self-expression, we were able to unearth the one-of-a-kind essence that lies dormant within us, and we gained the ability to navigate life with a revitalized sense of purpose and genuineness. The book "Awaken Inner Alchemy" sheds light on the route that leads to self-empowerment and reminds us that the limitless potential for personal development and self-actualization is latent inside each of us.

Finally, during the fourth phase of the Kindle Your Inner Drive process, we fanned the embers of our internal desire and propelled ourselves forward with unyielding determination. We became clearer about our passions, identified our purposeful intents, and developed techniques to keep the fire that burns within us going strong. We cultivated the strength and resilience to endure by surrounding ourselves with good influences, engaging in self-care practices, and enjoying even the tiniest wins. Kindle Your Inner Drive reminded us that the trip does not end when we reach the Peak; instead, it continues as we take the flame of our ambitions into the rest of the expanse that is our lives. It taught us that we have the potential to create a life of purpose and have a meaningful influence in the world around us if we connect our actions with our passions and remain true to who we are as individuals.

As we come to the end of this formative chapter, let us take the opportunity to reflect on the life-changing knowledge we've gained and make a concerted effort to incorporate it into our daily routines. The Peak has brought us to new heights of self-awareness, empathy, and creativity and kindled within us a burning desire to live a life of meaning and leave a legacy. This desire has not only brought us to new heights of self-awareness, but it has also brought us to new heights of creativity.

From this vantage position, we can take in a comprehensive view of our personal development, both the heights we have attained and the depths we have descended. The trip has not been without its difficulties and unknowns, but precisely through these tests, we have found true strength and tenacity within ourselves. We are here today as living proof of the incredible potential that lies dormant within every one of us.

As we say our goodbyes to the Peak and prepare to start a new chapter, let us remember to keep the spirit of metamorphosis alive within us. May we never stop puzzling over our viewpoints, delving into new sensory realms, reawakening our inner alchemy, and igniting our internal drive with undying zeal and commitment. And as we do so, let us not forget that the summit is not the end but a new beginning; it is a launching pad from which we can soar even higher, inspiring others with our wonderful adventure. So let us remember that as we reach the top, it is not the end but the beginning.

In conclusion, let us pay tribute to the transformative force of the Peak and rejoice in the phenomenal growth we have accomplished. Let us take the lessons and the transformation we have experienced as we begin the next chapter of our extraordinary lives. Let us do this with grateful hearts, minds that have been enlarged by newly discovered wisdom, and spirits that a sense of purpose has ignited. We pray that the Peak will always serve as a beacon of light, prompting us to recall that the ability to control our destinies and make an indelible imprint on the world lies within each of us.

This is not the end but rather the beginning of a remarkable adventure — a life filled with opportunities for development, exploration, and influence. Let us take courageous steps into the unknown, fully aware that our experience will indelibly alter us. As we move forward, let us acknowledge our great potential and prioritize to continue scaling new heights in terms of our development and awareness of ourselves.

As we prepare to turn the page and enter the next chapter of our incredible adventure, we find we are poised on the brink of profound discovery. The Peak has prepared us, sculpted us, and shed light on the route that leads to our most authentic selves. As we prepare to enter the section of the book titled "Legacy Unveiled: Leaving a Lasting Mark," we are encouraged to give some thought to the legacy we hope to leave behind, which is a demonstration of the difference we can make in the world and in the lives of the people we come into contact with.

In this chapter, we delve into the fundamental nature of our existence, which is the profound realization that the amount of time we spend on Earth is limited. Yet, the amount of impact we may have is virtually limitless. As we craft the story of our lives and set in motion a chain of events that is felt far beyond the confines of our travels, we investigate our thoughts, deeds, and decisions' influence. The game Legacy Unveiled encourages us to think about the legacy we want to leave behind, the stories we want to tell, and the impression we want to make on the canvas of humanity's history.

Within these pages, we will learn the essential components of a meaningful legacy that defies time constraints and impacts future generations' minds and hearts. In this discussion, we will investigate the idea that leaving a legacy is not just about doing great things but also about profoundly influencing the lives of other people and the world around us. The actual meaning of leaving a legacy behind can be found in the seemingly insignificant acts of charity and connection that we share with those who come after us, as well as in the core beliefs we implant in them.

We will work together to untangle the strands woven into the tapestry of an extraordinary heritage. We will find the latent potential within us to bring about long-lasting change, advocate for causes that are near and dear to our hearts, and inspire others through our actions. The book "Legacy Unveiled" compels us to look beyond the boundaries of our own lives and acknowledge the connectivity of the human experience we all have in common. In this tapestry, each thread helps to tell a different part of the emotional story of our shared heritage.

As we move forward into this new chapter, let us do so with a feeling of purpose and a profound awareness that our choices will impact the world we live in tomorrow. We pray that the many people throughout history who have left an indelible mark on human events may serve as a source of motivation, empowerment, and direction for us. And as we go deeper into the topic of legacies, may each of us take a moment to ponder our paths and how we might interweave our stories into the fabric of history.

The values we hold dear, our influence on others, and our impression of the world are all part of the legacy we leave behind; it is not confined to the accomplishments we have accomplished or the material possessions we have accumulated. Let us not be afraid to harness the power of our narrative, for within it lies the ability to leave a legacy that will reverberate in the minds and hearts of future generations. It is now time to reveal the splendor and importance of our heritage. This legacy will testify to our mission, passion, and unyielding determination to make a difference in the world.

Hello, and thank you for joining us here at "Legacy Unveiled: Leaving a Lasting Mark." Let us begin this profound journey together to shed light on the steps leading to a legacy that will outlast time and live on in the memories of those who follow in our footsteps.

Chapter 13

Legacy Unveiled: Leaving a Lasting Mark

You are invited to enter the **"Legacy Unveiled: Leaving a Lasting Mark"** world and experience the remarkable journey that awaits you. Together, with appreciation in our hearts, we set out on our adventure, shining a light on the road that will one day lead to a legacy that will echo through the centuries. Get ready to be fascinated as we reveal the holy steps that will carve an indelible footprint on the fabric of existence. Dive into the magic of this life-altering adventure and see the extraordinary force of a legacy that defies the limits of death by vibrating with meaning, insight, and the echoes of eternity.

Legacy is not about accumulating wealth or pursuing power. It is a far deeper idea that includes the essence of who we are and what we stand for. To properly comprehend and leave a legacy, we must begin with the basics, aligning our values and behaviors with the teachings of God's Word.

It is easy to lose sight of the genuine meaning of legacy in a world that often values material belongings and worldly achievements. It is judged not by the size of our money accounts or the titles we hold but by our impact on others and the ideals we instill in future generations.

Our relationship with God is the cornerstone of a lifelong legacy. We can lay a solid and unwavering foundation for our legacy by seeking His guidance, studying His Word, and aligning our lives with His teachings. This connection with God gives us insight, discernment, and a sense of purpose that transcends earthly interests.

God's Word gives us a plan for living a meaningful life and leaving a lasting impression. It teaches us the importance of love, compassion, forgiveness, and selflessness in leaving a legacy that reflects God's character. We can significantly impact those around us if we embrace these concepts and incorporate them into our daily lives.

It is not about self-promotion or personal benefit to leave a legacy. It is about helping others selflessly, using our God-given gifts and talents to uplift and inspire. It is about making a positive difference in the lives of those we meet, whether via acts of kindness, mentoring relationships, or spreading the message of God's love and salvation.

When we build our legacy on the tenets of God's Word, we are subject to principles that transcend the transient nature of this world. We recognize that true fulfillment comes from living a purposeful life and making a difference in the lives of others. We gain the strength and confidence to venture out of our comfort zones, take chances, and pursue undertakings that line with God's will via our faith in Him.

Building a legacy based on God's Word necessitates planning and a dedication to personal growth and transformation. It entails seeking wisdom and insight continuously, fostering virtues such as humility, integrity, and appreciation, and enabling the Holy Spirit to act in and through us. It is a lifelong journey that demands patience, resilience, and courageous faith.

We must remember that our influence extends beyond our immediate circle as we embark on this journey of legacy creation. It is not confined to our family, friends, or community but also to society as a whole and future generations. We are responsible for being agents of positive change, advocating for justice and righteousness, and being a light in a dark world.

We may face hurdles, disappointments, and times of doubt in our quest for a legacy. But we must remember that our confidence in God and His promises keep us going. His Word, Spirit, and constant love have given us all we need to leave a lasting legacy.

Let us deliberate in our actions, words, and relationships, understanding that every connection can affect someone else's life. Let us value character over accomplishments, influence over recognition, and love over worldly prosperity. Doing so can leave a permanent mark that shows God's love and impacts lives forever.

Finally, legacy is about something other than money or power. It is about the principles we uphold, the people we touch, and the difference we make. By constructing our legacy on the foundation of God's Word, we ensure that our activities follow His truth and intentions. Let us seize the chance to leave a lasting mark that honors God, inspires others, and bears witness to His faithfulness. May our legacy be a shining example of His love and grace for future generations.

When I reflect on the concept of legacy within my family, it is intertwined with the story of my hardworking father, who dedicated his life to providing for us. Growing up in a middle-class home, his primary focus was ensuring our financial security. However, there needed to be more in building deep relationships with his children and forging new friendships. As my father entered his sixties, he began facing health complications that would eventually claim his life in February 2022. During those final months, we had numerous conversations about his impending departure. He expressed his desire to ensure that my mother would be taken care of financially and that his four children would receive some form of inheritance. In his eyes, this was the epitome of leaving a legacy.

Yet, as his passing became a reality and we bid him farewell in a small funeral attended only by immediate family members, it dawned on me that while my father would forever live in my heart, his legacy would not have a lasting impact on others. It struck me that legacy is not solely about material possessions or financial security but rather about the positive influence we have on the lives of others. It encompasses the support, love, advice, and wisdom we impart to future generations.

In contrast to my father's legacy, my mother embodied the essence of leaving a lasting mark. An angel in human form, she consistently sought opportunities to help those in need. From my childhood to adulthood and even now, at 70 years old, she continues to assist others selflessly. I vividly recall an encounter at a store where a stranger recognized my mother and enthusiastically called out her name. Intrigued, I asked how they knew each other, and the person explained that my mother had gone to court with them, written letters to the judge, and ultimately significantly reduced their sentence. You see, my mother worked as a correctional officer. She later started her practice as a psychotherapist and has impacted the lives of countless individuals within the justice system and those who required her aid. Through her acts of compassion, she has created a legacy that will be remembered long after she leaves this earth.

As for myself, my journey toward understanding the importance of legacy began around six years ago during a discussion with an entrepreneur and CEO. He shared his inspiring story of starting his company from the basement, having migrated from Cuba with a deep passion for his work. However, what truly resonated with me was his genuine enjoyment of connecting with people. I was naturally drawn to him and his narrative, which sparked a newfound realization. Legacy was not merely about personal achievements or financial success but about the impact we have on the lives of others.

Motivated by this revelation, I immersed myself in the world of leadership and embraced the role of a servant leader. I found fulfillment in mentoring and coaching individuals who were navigating personal challenges. I organized technology boot camps, facilitated small groups, and engaged in various initiatives to make a positive difference. During this period, the concept of legacy took root in my heart and mind.

However, leaving a legacy is not limited to one's family or immediate circle of influence. I came to understand that it extended beyond personal achievements and accolades. It encompassed giving back to those in need and making a meaningful impact on society. In my pursuit of leaving a lasting legacy outside of my family, I am committed to continuing my efforts to uplift and support those around me.

Legacy is about more than leaving a financial inheritance; it is about creating a ripple effect of positivity and inspiration. It is about investing in others, touching lives, and empowering individuals to reach their full potential. Through acts of kindness, compassion, and mentorship, we can shape the lives of others and contribute to a better world.

Understand me; I'm not saying you should strive to leave a legacy to receive praise or admiration. It stems from the great joy of sharing in another person's development and developing a sense of pride in contributing to it. Whether our actions are celebrated publicly or go unnoticed, the heart of our legacy is the lives we have changed for the better.

Making a positive impact in the world is a primary motivation for setting out on the route to immortality. It's not about getting recognition or pats on the back but the inner joy of knowing that our efforts have helped another person grow and flourish.

When we see the people we have helped flourish and be happy, we experience particular satisfaction. It's an intangible emotion that money and praise can't buy. Instead, calm happiness comes from knowing we've improved someone else's life, even a little.

Consider the impact of a role model encouraging young people to pursue their goals. Seeing their mentees succeed is much more rewarding than any accolades or public acknowledgment a mentor might receive. Seeing the mentee grow is more satisfying than receiving any award or honor.

Similarly, we don't help others out of some desire to be hailed as heroes or for the praise that comes with it. Instead, a sincere desire to assist those in need, elevate them, and improve their lives drives it.

The satisfaction comes from making a difference, not receiving external validation for our efforts.

Building a legacy is about laying the groundwork for a community, always there for each other. Inspiring and enabling others to realize their most significant potential requires that we model those principles ourselves. By focusing our efforts on the joy, we get from witnessing the development of others; we may reject the false notion that we need others' approval to feel successful.

So, let's adjust our thinking and realize that the beauty of leaving a legacy is found in the genuine happiness and satisfaction we feel when we see the growth and transformation of others. It's about helping other people and taking comfort in knowing that even a tiny part of our lives has contributed to their success and fulfillment.

Not to take my word for it, but the concept of legacy has been ingrained in humanity's fabric since humanity's inception. It holds a profound meaning that transcends time and continues to resonate throughout generations. The Bible itself shares stories that exemplify the enduring nature of legacy, one of which is the story of Jesus Christ.

Jesus' legacy has endured for over two thousand years, impacting countless lives and shaping history. His teachings, acts of compassion, and sacrificial love left an indelible mark on the world. His legacy lives on through the Christian faith, serving as a guiding light for millions of believers.

The Bible, a testament to the power of legacy, contains numerous verses that speak to its significance. One such verse is found in **Proverbs 13:22**, which states, "A good man leaves an inheritance to his children's children, but the sinner's wealth is laid up for the righteous." This verse highlights that a legacy extends beyond one's lifetime, impacting future generations.

Another verse, **Ecclesiastes 7:1**, says, "A good name is better than fine perfume, and the day of death is better than the day of birth." This verse emphasizes the importance of the legacy we leave behind, suggesting that a life well-lived and a good reputation are more valuable than the mere accumulation of worldly possessions.

In the New Testament, the Apostle Paul speaks to the concept of legacy in his letter to Timothy. In **2 Timothy 2:2**, he writes, "And the things you have heard me say in the presence of many witnesses, entrust to reliable people who will also be qualified to teach others." Here, Paul encourages Timothy to pass on the teachings and wisdom he has received, creating a legacy that continues to impact future generations.

The story of Jesus himself exemplifies the transformative power of legacy. Through his teachings, miracles, and ultimate sacrifice on the cross, Jesus left a legacy of love, forgiveness, and redemption. His life and death continue to inspire and shape the lives of believers, fostering a legacy that transcends time and touches the hearts of individuals across generations.

Through these biblical narratives and teachings, we gain a deeper understanding of the significance of legacy. It is not merely about the accumulation of wealth or material possessions but rather about the impact we have on the lives of others and the values we instill in future generations.

According to the Bible, legacy is the practice of leaving a lasting impression through deeds of love, kindness, and wisdom sharing. It is about living a life that reflects our faith, values, and beliefs, inspiring others to follow in our footsteps and continue the legacy of hope, compassion, and transformation.

So, as we journey through life, let us strive to embrace the true essence of legacy. Let us be intentional in our actions, seeking to make a positive impact on those around us. By embodying the teachings of love, compassion, and forgiveness, we can leave behind a legacy that stands the test of time and brings light to future generations.

Let's step into a world where the extraordinary is possible, dreams take flight, and the legacy you leave behind becomes a masterpiece that transcends time. Welcome to a journey unlike any other that will ignite your imagination, stir your soul, and unveil the hidden magic within you. Just as Willy Wonka's Chocolate Factory promised wonder and enchantment, so does the path to creating your legacy. Prepare to embark on a whimsical adventure as we unlock the secrets to crafting a legacy that will leave the world in awe.

As the gates to this amazing realm swing open, you'll immerse yourself in a realm where endless possibilities and imagination knows no bounds. Picture a land where each step is paved with the shimmering dust of inspiration, and the air is infused with the sweet scent of ambition and purpose. Here, your legacy is not just a historical footnote but a grand symphony that resonates through the ages.

In this magical world, you'll discover the ten steps shaping your journey and guiding you in creating a legacy that defies expectations. These steps are not mere instructions but keys that unlock hidden chambers within your soul, unveiling the true potential that lies dormant within you. Each step is a portal to a realm of profound transformation, where you'll discover the power of connection, the art of giving, and the beauty of leaving a lasting impact.

With every turn of the page, you'll be whisked away on an enchanting adventure, encountering colorful characters, breathtaking landscapes, and heart-stirring moments of revelation. You'll witness the power of laughter as it echoes through the valleys, the joy of building bridges that unite communities, and the exhilaration of chasing dreams that dance in the sky.

Together, we'll delve into the secrets of crafting a legacy that transcends the ordinary. We'll explore the art of leaving footprints of adventure, igniting flames of inspiration, and celebrating the masterpiece that is your life. Each step will be a brushstroke on the canvas of your legacy, painting a picture that will awe and inspire generations to come.

So, hold your breath and enter a world where the extraordinary is possible. Let your heart be your guide as we embark on this remarkable journey. Embrace wonder, embrace magic, and brace yourself for the most incredible adventure—crafting a legacy that will leave the world breathless. Welcome to a realm where dreams come alive, imagination reigns supreme, and you hold the power to create a legacy that will be whispered in awe for eternity.

Step 1: Craft Your Legacy Blueprint - Imagine yourself as an architect designing a masterpiece. Take a colorful canvas and begin sketching your unique blueprint for your legacy. Consider the values, passions, and experiences that will shape your creation.

Step 2: Unleash Your Inner Artist - Embrace your creative side and unleash your inner artist. Paint your legacy with bold strokes of kindness, compassion, and joy. Use vibrant colors of love and inspiration to bring your masterpiece to life.

Step 3: Dance to Your Rhythm - Find your rhythm and let it guide you. Dance through life with grace and purpose, leaving a trail of inspiration in your wake. Let the world hear the beautiful melody of your legacy as you move to the beat of your drum.

Step 4: Scatter Seeds of Positivity - Become a gardener of positivity, planting seeds of encouragement and kindness wherever you go. Watch as your legacy blooms and blossoms, filling the world with beauty and joy.

Step 5: Write Your Story - Imagine yourself as a skilled wordsmith, penning the chapters of your life. Write a story that captivates hearts, inspires minds, and leaves a lasting impression. Let your words be a beacon of hope and wisdom for future generations.

Step 6: Build Bridges of Connection - Like a skilled engineer, build bridges of connection across generations. Strengthen the bonds of family, friendship, and community. Let these bridges be a testament to the power of unity and love.

Step 7: Embrace the Power of Laughter - Unleash the power of laughter and let it ripple through the halls of your legacy. Infuse joy and humor into your interactions, leaving people with smiles and warmth in their hearts.

Step 8: Weave Threads of Impact - Imagine yourself as a master weaver, intricately crafting a tapestry of impact. Weave threads of kindness, generosity, and service into the fabric of your legacy. Let each thread create a ripple effect that touches lives far and wide.

Step 9: Paint the Sky with Dreams - Be a dreamer, a visionary artist who paints the sky with dreams. Dream big and inspire others to do the same. Let your dreams soar high, igniting the sparks of ambition in the hearts of those around you.

Step 10: Leave Footprints of Adventure - Explore the world with a spirit of adventure, leaving footprints in the sands of time. Seek new experiences, embrace challenges, and push the boundaries of what is possible. Let your legacy be a testament to a life lived fully and fearlessly.

Remember, your legacy is a work of art that evolves and grows with every choice you make. Be bold, be daring, and embrace the creativity within you. Let your imagination soar as you craft a vibrant, dynamic, and unique legacy.

As you reflect on the steps you've taken to build your legacy, you can't help but feel a sense of fulfillment and pride. You've embraced your creativity, spread positivity, and made meaningful connections. Your journey has been filled with laughter, impact, and dreams that have painted the sky with vibrant colors. Your footprints of adventure have left an indelible mark on the world, and you've become a beacon of inspiration for those around you.

But as you delve deeper into the concept of legacy, you realize that it's not all sunshine and rainbows. A dark side lurks beneath the surface – the seductive allure of power and money. In pursuing success, it's easy to get caught up in the web of divisions and corruption that taints the very essence of legacy.

As you conclude your exploration of Chapter 13, the essence of legacy lingers in the air. You've witnessed the profound impact of leaving a positive mark on the world, and your heart is filled with a deep sense of purpose. But before you turn the page to Chapter 14, take a moment to reflect on the journey you've embarked upon.

Throughout this chapter, you've uncovered the power of legacy and the remarkable ways it can shape lives for generations to come.

From crafting your unique blueprint to embracing the power of laughter, you've discovered that legacy is not merely about material wealth or achievements but about the lasting imprint we leave on others.

But as you move forward, it is crucial to acknowledge that legacy is not immune to the dark forces that can threaten its very essence. **In Chapter 14: The Dark Side of Power and Money: Confronting Divisions and Corruption,** a new chapter awaits one that shines a light on the shadowy underbelly that plagues our society.

This chapter opens a gateway to a world where greed, manipulation, and unethical practices threaten to undermine the very foundations of legacy. It takes you on a journey that will challenge your beliefs and shed light on the uncomfortable truths that often go unnoticed. Prepare to confront the dark side that can taint even the noblest of legacy.

Chapter 14

The Dark Side of Power and Money: Confronting Divisions and Corruption

As we venture into Chapter 14, we find ourselves standing at the crossroads of a world engulfed in the destructive grip of power and money. It is a realm where the pursuit of personal gain often takes precedence over the welfare of the people and where corruption and division flourish. This chapter will deeply explore society's dark underbelly, shedding light on the insidious forces that drive greed, manipulation, and unethical practices broken out into five sections below.

Section 1: Unmasking the Illusions

In the first section, we peel back the layers of illusion and unveil the true nature of power and money. We delve into the mechanisms through which these forces shape our world and analyze the tactics employed to maintain control and influence. From political maneuverings to corporate agendas, we expose the web of deceit that ensnares society, hindering progress and perpetuating injustice."

Real-Life Situation 1: Political Corruption and Manipulation

Let's examine a real-life situation highlighting power and money's dark side: political corruption and manipulation. We explore how individuals and groups in positions of authority exploit their positions for personal gain, disregarding the well-being and interests of the people they are meant to serve. Through in-depth research and compelling examples, we reveal the intricate webs of influence, bribery, and manipulation that taint the political landscape.

For example:

a. It is the rampant corruption within some developing countries, where leaders siphon off public funds for personal enrichment, leaving their nations impoverished and their citizens suffering. One such case is the kleptocracy in Nigeria, where corrupt politicians and officials embezzle billions of dollars for public services and development projects. This diversion of funds hinders economic progress, exacerbates poverty, and undermines the population's well-being.
b. In the corporate world, the case of Enron stands as a stark example of corporate greed and manipulation. Enron, once considered one of the largest and most innovative energy companies, collapsed in 2001 due to fraudulent accounting practices and deceptive financial reporting. Executives at Enron used complex schemes to hide debt and inflate profits, misleading investors and employees alike. The fallout from the scandal resulted in significant financial losses for many and led to increased scrutiny of corporate governance and accounting practices.

These examples demonstrate how power and money can be wielded for personal gain, at the expense of the greater good. They reveal the lengths to which individuals and organizations may go to manipulate systems and institutions to serve their own interests. By examining these real-life situations, we gain insight into the dark side of power and money and the devastating consequences that can arise when ethical boundaries are crossed.

Real-Life Situation 2: Corporate Greed and Exploitation

Now we turn our attention to the realm of corporate power and money. We shed light on the practices of large corporations that prioritize profits over ethical considerations and the welfare of their employees and the environment. Through eye-opening case studies, we expose labor exploitation, environmental degradation, and unethical business practices. By examining these real-life situations, we aim to raise awareness about the consequences of unchecked corporate power and the urgent need for responsible business practices.

For example:

    a. One prominent example of corporate power and money influencing unethical practices is the case of the Rana Plaza factory collapse in Bangladesh. In 2013, a multi-story garment factory complex collapsed, resulting in the tragic loss of over 1,100 lives and injuring thousands of workers. The incident brought international attention to the exploitative working conditions and safety violations prevalent in the global fashion industry. Many major clothing brands were implicated in the tragedy, as they had outsourced their production to factories like Rana Plaza, where workers endured long hours, low wages, and hazardous working conditions. This case highlighted the dark side of corporate supply chains, exposing the human cost of cheap labor and profit-driven practices.

    b. Additionally, we can examine the practices of large pharmaceutical companies that prioritize profits over public health.

The opioid crisis in the United States, for example, revealed how some pharmaceutical companies aggressively marketed and distributed highly addictive pain medications, contributing to widespread addiction and devastating consequences for individuals and communities. The pursuit of profit led to the overprescription and misuse of opioids, causing immense human suffering and straining healthcare systems. This case underscores the dangerous consequences of prioritizing financial gain over the well-being and safety of individuals.

By exploring these real-life situations and delving into the complex dynamics of corporate power and money, we understand our challenges in creating a more ethical and responsible business environment. Through critical analysis and thought-provoking examples, we aim to expose the consequences of unchecked corporate practices, encourage dialogue, and inspire change. We aim to empower individuals and communities to demand accountability and advocate for responsible business practices prioritizing people and the planet. Only by shining a light on these issues and working collectively can we begin to address the dark side of corporate power and money and create a more equitable and sustainable future.

Section 2: The Fallout of Corruption

Moving forward, we confront the devastating consequences of unchecked greed and corruption. We examine how power imbalances and the insatiable desire for wealth lead to the exploitation of vulnerable individuals and communities. Through thought-provoking case studies and real-life examples, we explore the profound impact of corruption on social, economic, and environmental landscapes, leaving no stone unturned in our quest for truth.

For example:

a. One poignant example of the fallout of corruption is the case of the 1Malaysia Development Berhad (1MDB) scandal in Malaysia. This massive financial scandal involved the misappropriation of billions of dollars from the state investment fund, 1MDB, by high-level officials and their associates. The stolen funds were used for personal gain, including luxury real estate, artwork, and extravagant parties. The scandal highlighted the corruption within the Malaysian government and revealed the devastating impact on the country's economy and its people. The misappropriated funds could have addressed pressing social issues like poverty alleviation, infrastructure development, and education. Instead, they were siphoned off for personal enrichment, leaving a trail of economic instability and public disillusionment.
b. Martin Shkreli: Martin Shkreli gained infamy as the "Pharma Bro" for his role in the pharmaceutical industry. Shkreli founded Turing Pharmaceuticals and acquired the rights to a life-saving drug called Daraprim. He then raised the drug's price from $13.50 to $750 per pill overnight, sparking outrage and public scrutiny. Shkreli's unscrupulous actions highlighted the profit-driven nature of the pharmaceutical industry and the negative impact it can have on vulnerable patients.

Section 3: Divisions that Divide Us

In this section, we confront the deep divisions plaguing our society, fueled by the pursuit of power and wealth accumulation. We probe into how these divisions manifest through systemic inequalities, socio-economic disparities, or discriminatory practices. By shining a light on the root causes of division, we aim to ignite a collective awakening that propels us toward unity and solidarity.

For example:

   a. **Income Inequality:** The wealth gap between the rich and the poor is a significant source of division in many societies. High-income earners often have greater access to opportunities, resources, and privileges, while those with lower incomes struggle to meet their basic needs. This divide can lead to social tensions, resentment, and injustice.
   b. **Racial and Ethnic Discrimination:** Power and money can perpetuate racial and ethnic divisions. Discriminatory practices, such as unequal access to employment, housing, and education, can reinforce inequalities based on race or ethnicity. This division can create deep-seated societal divisions, fueling resentment and hindering social progress.
   c. **Political Polarization:** Power struggles and money's political influence can exacerbate divisions between political ideologies. Pursuing power and financial gain can lead to prioritizing partisan interests over the common good. This can result in a lack of cooperation, gridlock, and a widening divide between political factions.
   d. **Social Class Divisions:** Wealth and social status can create divisions between different social classes. The accumulation of power and money by a privileged few can lead to the exclusion and marginalization of those from lower socioeconomic backgrounds. This division can contribute to social unrest, class struggles, and a lack of social mobility.

Section 4: Voices of Resistance

Amidst the darkness, we encounter beacons of hope and resilience—individuals and communities that refuse to be silenced by the forces of power and money. In this section, we amplify their voices, sharing stories of those who have risen against corruption and worked tirelessly to bring about meaningful change. Their journeys inspire us to take a stand, challenge the status quo, and forge a path towards a more just and equitable world.

For example:

a. **Greta Thunberg:** Greta Thunberg, a young Swedish environmental activist, has become a prominent voice in the fight against climate change. Through her passionate speeches and global activism, she has inspired millions to act and demand urgent measures to address the environmental crisis.
b. **Malala Yousafzai:** Malala Yousafzai is a Pakistani activist advocating girls' education. Despite facing threats and violence from the Taliban, she continues to fight for educational rights and empower girls worldwide through her Malala Fund.
c. **Nelson Mandela:** Nelson Mandela, the late South African leader, and Nobel Peace Prize laureate, dedicated his life to dismantling the apartheid system and promoting racial reconciliation. His commitment to justice, equality, and peace has made him an icon of resilience and forgiveness.
d. **The #MeToo Movement:** The #MeToo movement, sparked by activist Tarana Burke and amplified by countless survivors, has shed light on the prevalence of sexual harassment and assault. This collective movement has given a voice to survivors, held perpetrators accountable, and initiated a global conversation about gender-based violence.

Section 5: Confronting the Status Quo

As we near the culmination of this chapter, we call upon readers to confront the status quo and question the prevailing narratives dictated by power and money. We explore strategies for dismantling corrupt systems, fostering transparency, and holding those in positions of authority accountable. Through empowering individuals and communities, we believe in our collective capacity to reshape the narrative and build a more inclusive and just society.

For example:

a. **Edward Snowden:** Edward Snowden, a former intelligence officer, exposed the mass surveillance programs of the United States government. His whistleblowing actions shed light on the erosion of privacy rights and ignited a global debate on the balance between national security and individual liberties.
b. **Ai Weiwei:** Ai Weiwei, a Chinese artist, and activist, uses his art and public platform to challenge the authoritarian regime in China. Through his provocative installations and social media presence, he brings attention to human rights issues, freedom of expression, and government censorship.
c. **Youth Activists:** Young activists such as Emma Gonzalez and David Hogg, survivors of the Parkland school shooting in Florida, have been instrumental in advocating for stricter gun control measures. Their passionate activism and powerful speeches have galvanized a generation and sparked a nationwide conversation on gun violence prevention.
d. **Investigative Journalists:** Journalists like Glenn Greenwald, Amy Goodman, and Seymour Hersh have dedicated their careers to exposing corruption, government misconduct, and corporate malfeasance. Their investigative reporting holds those in power accountable and provides the public with crucial information to challenge the status quo.

In our quest for better lifestyles, we must confront the harsh reality of living in a world where power and money are the driving forces. We witness these forces' enormous inequalities, pervasive injustices, and harmful influence over our lives. It has the potential to be discouraging, leaving us with a sense that we have no control, that we are detached, and that we crave change. I would like you to permit me to remind you, my fellow individuals looking for a better future, that the potential to change our lives and the world around us is within everyone.

It's time to free ourselves from societal norms, false worldviews, and the notion that the sum of our bank accounts or titles determines our value. We must reject the narratives that foster divisiveness, help corruption thrive, and limit our lives to meaninglessness. It is time to reestablish a connection with our true selves, reclaim our power, and pave a new way forward for ourselves.

Imagine a future in which power and money are used as instruments for collective well-being, and success is not defined by personal gain but rather by the beneficial impact we make on the lives of others. Imagine a culture in which we are guided in our actions by empathy, compassion, and justice; a society in which relationships are valued; and a culture in which the pursuit of a better life is inextricably linked to the well-being of those in our immediate environment.

We must start by looking inward at ourselves to bring about this transition. Our conceptions of success, worth, and happiness have been influenced by deeply ingrained beliefs and training, which must be questioned and challenged. It must have the guts to examine our goals, motivations, and biases. We can rediscover our genuine principles and restore our authentic selves if we can see through the deceptions that power and wealth have perpetrated upon us.

We can rethink what it means to be successful now that we have this additional insight. It is not about amassing riches for its own sake; instead, it is about employing our resources to elevate other people, create opportunities for those who have been disadvantaged, and address the urgent concerns that threaten the well-being of our planet and its inhabitants. It is about establishing a legacy rooted in love, compassion, and the pursuit of justice rather than in accumulating worldly possessions. This legacy extends beyond the realm of material possessions.

Together, we can challenge the established order and make those in authoritative positions answer for their actions. We can reject the role of mere bystanders and uninvolved beneficiaries of the decisions made by a small minority. We become agents of transformation when we actively develop our communities, participate in grassroots movements, and advocate for change.

But let us not overlook that change starts within each of us and then spreads outside. We can bring about significant shifts through the simple yet meaningful exchanges we have with one another, the acts of kindness we perform, and the level of empathy we maintain. We may encourage others to challenge the dominant narratives and work toward a more just and peaceful society by cultivating genuine connections with one another, lending a helpful hand, and listening with an open heart.

This path will be full of its share of difficulties. It will require fortitude, determination, and a willingness to confront our prejudices and privileges to be successful. However, when faced with challenges, let us draw strength from the fact that we are not the only ones going through them. We are part of a group, a community of people who share similar values and beliefs, and we are adamantly opposed to maintaining the status quo.

Therefore, my close companions, I invite you to join me on this life-altering adventure. Let us encourage one another, help one another rise above our circumstances, and be accountable to one another. Let us work together to build inclusive settings in which every person's opinion is taken seriously, cherished, and respected. Let us join in our shared vision of a future in which power and money serve the greater good, build bridges across the differences that separate us, and care for the wounds that we have suffered.

Although the path that lies ahead may be difficult, the capacity for making significant progress is present within every one of us. We can mold not just our own lives but also the lives of those around us and set in motion a chain reaction of positive transformation that will echo through future generations. As a community, let us kindle a fire of hope, compassion, and justice that blazes brightly and leads us to the better life we deserve. The moment has come to make a shift.

It is a waste of one's brief existence to spend it conforming one's behavior to the standards and expectations of society. We must recognize and celebrate our uniqueness to pave our way in a world that frequently attempts to classify and categorize us. This path to freedom demands bravery, introspection, and a willingness to question the established order to be traveled successfully.

We are socialized early to behave according to societal standards and expectations. It is up to society to tell us how we should act, how we should present ourselves, and what we ought to strive for. Messages dictating our worth based on characteristics such as income looks, and social position are constantly being thrown at us, and they are everywhere. It is simple to slip into the trap of living a life dominated by these norms, merely going through the motions without genuinely considering their validity or impact on one's life.

However, at the core of our beings resides a yearning for something greater. a strong desire for genuineness, completeness, and direction in life. We long to be untethered from the shackles that hold us captive to a reality that does not necessarily correspond with who we are. We all have a deep-seated desire to live a meaningful life where we can make the most of our strengths, skills, and interests.

To defy these standards and move into our truth requires a certain amount of bravery. It demands us to evaluate the systems and institutions that perpetuate the narratives critically passed down to us and call into question the stories that have been told. It means unlearning the limiting ideas that have kept us from moving forward and adopting a mindset open to possibilities and growth.

We make room for personal development, self-discovery, and nurturing our distinctive voice when we liberate ourselves from the limits of conventional norms and standards. We start to view life as an exciting journey, one in which we investigate the things that interest us, work toward realizing our ambitions and have a beneficial effect on the world around us. When the expectations of others no longer constrain us, we can become the architects of our destinies.

Living not by society's expectations does not mean ignoring rules or duties. It is about deciding which standards and expectations coincide with our core beliefs and goals and which norms and expectations we are willing to question or disobey. It is about recognizing our truth and letting that truth direct the choices we make and the things we do.

When we break free from society's constraints, we expose ourselves to the risk of being rejected and experiencing failure. It takes the ability to bounce back from setbacks and the determination to carry on regardless of the obstacles. However, it is through the difficulties that we face that we can learn, grow, and uncover our full potential and capabilities. We take on the role of trailblazers, blazing our trails and leaving behind our own legacy.

We must surround ourselves with a supportive group as we travel toward emancipation. We require the inspiration and insight of individuals who have traveled roads like ours or who have faith in the potential of our plan. As we venture into the unexplored realms of authentic life, these relationships provide motivation, direction, and a sense of belonging.

Self-care and self-reflection should be given the highest priority as we work toward living a life that deviates from the standards set by society. Taking the time to get to know ourselves, our core beliefs, and the things we aspire to achieve enables us to make decisions congruent with our true selves and do so intentionally. When we take the time to be still and reflect on our lives, we can see more clearly and acquire more profound insight into the direction we want our lives to take.

The trip of living a life that is outside of what is considered normal by society is not an easy journey, but it is a journey that should be taken. It is a voyage of self-discovery, personal development, and the attainment of empowerment. It is a path that enables us to live a life that is true to ourselves, has a purpose, and is fulfilled. And it is a journey that can inspire others to do the same thing, creating a ripple effect of liberty and transformation.

Therefore, let us acknowledge the value of this short life and the transience of this moment in time. Let us muster the intestinal fortitude to break free from the shackles of conventional expectations and live a life that is authentic to who we are as individuals. Let's work together to leave a legacy that reflects our contributions, passions, and ideals. By doing so, we improve our lives and encourage others to do the same, igniting a collective movement toward a society where everyone can live their truth and pursue their dreams.

As we bring this chapter 14 to a close, we stand at a pivotal moment in our journey. We have delved into the dark side of power and money, uncovering the divisions and corruption that plague our society. But now, it is time to shift our focus towards a path of healing and unity.

Chapter 15

Breaking the Chains: A Call to Action

We'll be answering that ringing "Call to Action" by pulling back the curtain on the Puppet Master in this chapter. Your transformational journey has allowed you to see, illuminating the hidden bonds that once held you prisoner like a puppet on a string controlled by the Puppet Master. You won't have to fumble in the dark, following false leads. Now is the time to put this Puppet Master under the microscope and expose him in the most obvious way imaginable.

A shadowy figure, the Puppet Master, works deftly behind the scenes to shape the world to their liking. He lures people into evil plots by preying on their base instincts and weaknesses. His rule extends over many decades and centuries, and the strife he sows has consequences for all of humankind.

This shadowy character uses the aspirations of individuals wanting power, fame, or riches to further his nefarious ends. He picks out people vulnerable to persuasion and then uses their vulnerabilities and anxieties against them.

The Puppet Master is an expert illusionist who makes it difficult for his victims to tell fact from fiction. He spins narratives that make them think they're acting freely when, in truth, they're just dancing to the tune of his master plan.

The use of terror is his primary tactic. The Puppet Master uses people's fears against them, making them feel helpless and unsafe. His puppets are unquestioning of orders since they were raised in such an atmosphere.

The Puppet Master is also skilled at exploiting love, devotion, and personal ties as tools of emotional manipulation. He uses emotional attachments to manipulate his victims into doing what he wants without them even realizing it's happening.

This manipulator feeds off social tensions, fanning the flames of bigotry and prejudice. By sowing discord, he keeps the climate fertile for manipulation and guarantees his authority will not be questioned.

We'll be answering that ringing "Call to Action" by pulling back the curtain on the Puppet Master in this chapter. Your transformational journey has allowed you to see, illuminating the hidden bonds that once held you prisoner like a puppet on a string controlled by the Puppet Master. You won't have to fumble in the dark, following false leads. Now is the time to put this Puppet Master under the microscope and expose him in the most obvious way imaginable.

He employs cunning and strategy in placing his marionettes in positions of authority and influence. He conceals himself in the shadows while executing his plans, which involve using their role and the resources they provide. These helpless victims are used as instruments in the vast orchestration conducted by the Puppet Master.

Despite the desolate landscape that the Puppet Master has portrayed, a glimmer of hope can be seen in the shadows. Resistance is starting to grow as more and more people become aware of the Puppet Master's power. Pursuing the truth becomes more intense, gradually reducing the puppeteer's level of control.

The line between influence and manipulation can often be blurry in our increasingly interconnected society, where the tendrils of social media reach into the most intimate parts of our lives. It might be challenging to identify the puppeteer's threads in a culture that values fast pleasure, and knee-jerk responses, where patience appears to be in short supply and anger is an all too frequent guest. This is especially true in a society that celebrates hasty replies.

Nevertheless, a spark of defiance may still be seen shining through this maelstrom of gloom. Certain people in the world defy the puppeteer's influence and refuse to play a passive role in the master's magnificent orchestration. These courageous spirits constantly question, challenge, and fight for a world liberated from oppressive chains and hidden restrictions. They are the change agents, the bearers of illumination, and they dare to rise against the domination of the puppeteer.

This intricate background of lying and trickery provides the setting for the story of Dennis, which is told against this backdrop. Dennis, a typical person, has unwittingly become involved in the intricate game of control that the puppeteer is playing. Dennis starts to question the sincerity of his views, the genuineness of his connections, and his place in this giant tapestry as the influence of the puppeteer continues to creep closer and closer into the picture. This impact is enhanced through various social media outlets. His journey is one of self-awareness, tenacity, and independence.

Dennis is prepared with a strong foundation in the Word of God, the understanding that creating and nurturing relationships is essential, and the commitment to follow 'The LIGHT Pathway.' As a result of his adoption of these guiding principles, he now finds that he is ready to tackle the difficulties within himself, which is the initial step toward transformation.

As his story progresses, Dennis draws power from this mysterious concoction. God's Word guides Dennis as he struggles with doubts about his faith, relationships, and identity brought on by the puppeteer's influence, which spreads through social media. He is finding stability in his relationships with those closest to him. And in his dedication to The LIGHT Pathway, he discovers the map that will lead him out of the maze of control and manipulation.

Dennis's path is more than just a self-improvement process; it has far-reaching consequences for himself and the people he cares about. The people closest to him feel the effects of the changes he goes through as he works through the difficulties within himself. By setting an example of the behavior he hopes to see more of, he encourages people around him to reject the puppet master's influence.

By resisting pervasive control and manipulation, especially on social media, this act of personal transformation becomes a catalyst for change. Dennis, who was once only a pawn in the puppeteer's game, is now a symbol of defiance. His life shows the power of God's Word, the importance of relationships, and the worth of walking The LIGHT Pathway. His resiliency to question inspires others and challenges the powers that be.

In other words, my reader, be ready to go on a deep dive into the world of manipulation, where the tricks of the trade and the mastermind behind it will be revealed. Following Dennis's footsteps, we will investigate options for breaking free from the puppeteer's control and asserting our independence. This path, illuminated by The LIGHT Pathway and directed by the divine Word, will test our mettle, spark our inner strength, and set the stage for a future free from the shackles of manipulation. This will help us see that the change we seek must occur within ourselves before it can spread to our communities and the world.

A Call to Action (5 Steps)

As we confront the puppet master's hold on humanity and rally together in a united front to break free from their grasp. It is a chapter of empowerment, resilience, and the unwavering determination to create a world free from manipulation and control.

1.) Unmasking the Puppet Master:

First and foremost, we must keep shining a light on the puppet master's deceptive control methods. We may gain greater understanding and power by learning more about their processes. We must expose the mastermind behind the curtain and bring down their web of lies and manipulation.

The only way out of the puppet master's grip is by unveiling their shady methods and illuminating their manipulative tactics. We can become immune to their sway only if we fortify ourselves with the ultimate weapon: information. We can better fight, counter, and deconstruct their schemes if we have a firm grasp on their mode of operation.

We must plunge headfirst into the ominous maze the puppet master has created to accomplish this. You'll need to devote much time and energy to research, thinking, and discovery. To properly understand the puppet master's ways, we must pay close attention to detail and be unrelenting in our pursuit of the truth.

To unmask the puppet master, one must do more than expose their identity. It's about drawing attention to their genuine goals, often masked by diversionary tactics. Only by peeling back these layers can the true nature of their strategy—one based on lies, deception, and control—be revealed.

We can expose their true identities and network of lies once we do so. This is no easy feat, as the puppet master's web is intricate, vast, and firmly embedded in our culture. However, we can start to unravel its components piece by piece if we have enough insight and understanding. The puppet master's power is weakened, and this process frees those trapped within it.

A.) Strategy to Unmask the Puppet Master:

- **Empowering Through God's Word:** Integrating our faith and God's Word into our lives more deeply might help us develop a sense of right and wrong. This spiritual protection might keep us from being swayed and direct our activities.

- **Education and Awareness:** Recognizing the methods used by the puppet master is the first step in exposing him. Learning their manipulative methods, strategies, and routines is essential. You can improve by reading, researching, attending seminars, and talking to others. Particularly in the digital sphere, where strategies vary swiftly, it is vital to stay abreast of the most recent ways of manipulation.
- **Critical Thinking:** Foster an atmosphere of doubt and inquiry. We need to create a culture where people feel comfortable challenging the current quo and the stories they're told. By exercising our critical thinking skills, we may separate reality from fantasy and see through the puppeteer's mask.
- **Promote Open Dialogue and Communication:** Providing venues for frank dialogue is essential. Conversations like these might help reveal covert intentions and challenge accepted wisdom. The puppet master's tricks can be uncovered if people talk to one another and share what they've noticed.
- **Building Strong Relationships:** A solid network of family and friends can help you through tough times. The people in this group can act as a support system, validating our experiences and providing new insights on spotting manipulation.

2.) Awakening the Collective Consciousness:

More than just personal fortitude and insight, we need a widespread awakening to escape the puppet master's complex web. A single flame can be extinguished, but when many gather, they form a beacon that can't be hidden. When this kind of group awareness is sparked, it can expose even the most covert forms of control and manipulation.

Therefore, we must stoke this common fire in each person's soul. We must serve as catalysts, fanning the flame of consciousness into a self-sustaining blaze. Though it may begin with one person, this flame has the potential to engulf the entire community.

To oppose the effect of a manipulative entity, it is necessary, albeit difficult, to awaken the collective consciousness. Here are several methods that can be used to spark this cultural realization.

A.) Strategy to Awaken the Collective Consciousness:

- **Storytelling and Artistic Expression:** Use literature, the visual and performing arts, music, and film as tools for education and thought reform. Art can potentially expose manipulation and open a conversation about critical social concerns.
- **Technology and Social Media Engagement:** Using digital resources like social media to reach more people. Make something that gets people thinking critically about manipulation techniques while keeping them interested. Promote group effort through internet campaigns, viral challenges, and trending hashtags.
- **Community Projects:** Start initiatives that bring people together in the neighborhood. Manipulation and collective consciousness may be explored in various contexts, including church small groups, public forums, discussion groups, and even community art initiatives.
- **Mindfulness and Self-reflection Activities:** Encourage people to engage in self-reflection and mindfulness practices like yoga, journaling, and meditation. These can improve self-awareness, making people less vulnerable to deception.
- **Gamification:** Make challenges, games, or contests that teach people about deception and how to avoid manipulation. This method can make education more exciting and enjoyable, attracting more students.

3.) Building Solidarity and Unity:

Conflict and unrest serve the puppet master's purposes. We must establish a link of togetherness and solidarity to oppose their sway. By recognizing our common humanity and welcoming those different from us, we may become an unstoppable force in the fight against deception and exploitation. By joining forces, we can make our calls for justice and transparency heard loud and clear.

Our greatest weapon is our strength in solidarity and unity in a world where the puppet master profits from separation, disunity, and discontent. The puppet master's schemes aim to separate people from one another, to make them feel alone and helpless. However, when we stand together, recognizing our common humanity and variety, we become an unstoppable force incapable of manipulation or exploitation.

To be united does not imply conformity. It calls for us to appreciate and value one another's unique qualities while acknowledging the common ground of our shared humanity. We should not see our differences as something to be exploited but rather as something to be celebrated. It strengthens our ability to work together, gives us more skills to resist exploitation, and broadens our perspective.

Solidarity strengthens this fellowship. It helps us understand one another, boosts friendships, and unites us. We can face misfortune together, help each other rise above it, and stand firm against the puppet master's attempts to drive a wedge between us. Together, we can't be defeated by those who would create conflict and division.

And when we stand together, we can raise our voices to hold those in authority accountable. When we speak as one, our demands for fairness and openness carry more weight, and we must be considered.

Building solidarity and unity is essential in confronting the puppet master. **Here are some innovative strategies:**

A.) Strategy for Building Solidarity and Unity:

- **Shared Activities:** Organize activities or events that promote community engagement and allow individuals to interact personally.
- **Diversity and Inclusion Training:** Offer workshops or training sessions that promote understanding different cultures, viewpoints, and experiences. Emphasize the importance of diversity and inclusivity in building a strong, united community.
- **Conflict Resolution Mechanisms:** Establish mechanisms for resolving disagreements respectfully and constructively. By addressing issues openly and fairly, you can prevent divisions from forming and maintain unity within the group.
- **Common Goals:** Identify common objectives or issues everyone in the community cares about. Working towards a shared goal can foster a sense of solidarity and unity, making the group more resilient to manipulation.
- **Effective Communication Channels:** Ensure open communication lines within the group. This allows for transparent dialogue, encourages active participation from everyone, and strengthens the sense of community.

4.) Cultivating Emotional Resilience:

The strength of a fortress lies not only in its walls and moats but also in the determination and preparedness of its defenders. Similarly, our fortress in the war against the puppet master is our emotional fortitude. It protects us from being manipulated, helps us persevere when things are tough, and guides us when we feel confused.

When we train ourselves to be emotionally resilient, we aren't just protecting ourselves against the puppet master's tricks; we're also making a long-term investment in our happiness. A strong sense of identity and emotional stability makes us more resilient to life's challenges and less vulnerable to control.

The process of growth relies heavily on introspection. It acts as a reflective surface through which we can analyze our innermost thoughts and reactions. We might lessen our susceptibility to the puppet master's manipulations by being more self-aware of our emotional triggers, strengths and weaknesses, and anxieties and insecurities. When we take the time to reflect on our own lives, we are better able to learn from our mistakes and adapt to the stresses of daily life.

Taking care of oneself is crucial in building up one's emotional fortitude. It's a good reminder that self-care is essential and that putting one's own needs first is acceptable. Emotional well-being is greatly aided by self-care routines including doing things we enjoy, being attentive, eating healthily, and getting plenty of sleep. They have a healing effect, relieving us of tension and stress and reviving us on all levels.

Here are some strategies for Building Strategy for Cultivating Emotions:

A.) Strategy for Cultivating Emotional:

- **Nurture Supportive Relationships:** Fill your life with upbeat, encouraging people. Having many friends by your side can help you feel less lonely, boost your confidence, and help you weather life's storms better.
- **Learn Healthy Coping Strategies:** Identify and manage your emotional triggers. These may be anything from writing in a journal to consulting a therapist to talking to a close friend. Learning to cope with emotional stress in healthy ways can significantly improve resilience.
- **Cultivate Optimism and Gratitude:** Try to keep a sunny disposition and focus on the positive aspects of your life. Maintaining a positive outlook and strong emotional fortitude in adversity can be enhanced by actively seeking reasons for gratitude.

5.) Disrupting the Narrative:

The puppet master manipulates our thoughts and behaviors in much the same way as a skilled storyteller. Their stories are crafted to keep them in power and advance their goals for as long as possible. Stopping the spread of these false stories is essential to freeing ourselves from their control.

Challenging the stories we've been told is the first step in creating disruption. This calls for an analytical mindset that questions the status quo and actively seeks out new points of view. Realizing that there are always two sides to every story and that the truth is usually in between the two is essential. Analyzing the puppet master's stories can help us understand their prejudices, goals, and control methods.

However, more is needed to challenge the narratives; we must also oppose them with different perspectives. To accomplish this, we must consult various materials, from printed books and magazines to online podcasts and video documentaries. By reading widely, we can learn about new perspectives, grasp complex arguments, and challenge the puppet master's propaganda.

Additionally, we need to give a platform to the underrepresented. The narratives of the puppet master exclude certain people, their stories, and their points of view. We need to give these people a bigger platform, giving due recognition to their knowledge and experiences. This not only promotes a more open and diverse conversation but also breaks the narratives of the puppet master.

Finally, we need to stop feeding the echo chambers that the puppet master uses to maintain power. By silencing opposition and encouraging conformity, echo chambers strengthen the narratives of the puppet master. Disrupting these echo chambers and cultivating a more open and informed collective awareness requires us to move outside our comfort zones, engage with individuals who believe differently, and challenge our ideas.

Here are some strategies for Building Strategy for Cultivating Emotions:

A.) Strategy for Disrupting the Narrative:

- Start with you: If you want to make significant changes, you must first try to alter your behavior. Understanding one's assumptions, prejudices, and habits is the first step in challenging accepted narratives. Pose difficult questions to yourself, examine your behaviors and their underlying motivations, and make principled choices.
- In a Larger Way, create a Revolutionary Podcast: Podcasts are quickly becoming a mainstream medium for disseminating information and ideas. Launch a podcast that questions accepted wisdom by featuring voices from underrepresented communities.
- Virtual Debates and Panels: Set up virtual roundtable discussions and debates intending to debunk commonly held beliefs. The worldwide reach of media like social media and video conferencing means that more voices worldwide may be heard and considered.

Embarking on the Path to Action:

Action, not observation, is required to break the puppet master's shackles. This enlightenment must be translated into action to move us forward toward transformation. In this struggle, activism, advocacy, and community organizing are powerful instruments that can bring about sea changes, what we do matters, whether it's nonviolent protest, supporting local projects, or holding the powerful accountable.

In the final moments of this chapter, we make an impassioned plea for change. This rallying cry speaks to everyone's deep-seated desire to break free of the puppeteer. We call on you to reclaim your independence, push back against the narratives imposed upon us, and work toward a world where power is balanced by empathy, compassion, and justice.

We can free ourselves and the next generation from manipulation if we work together to shatter these figurative chains. Doing so charts a future where honesty, agency, and solidarity characterize the human condition. This is the rallying cry, the lighthouse beckoning each of us to take the courageous first step toward our freedom as a group.

Conclusion

In conclusion, as we reach the end of this extraordinary journey, it is time to reflect on the profound lessons we have learned and the transformative power within each of us. We set out on this path to expose the harmful worldviews that have held humanity captive, and in doing so, we have shed light on the unseen chains that bind us.

Through our exploration, we have unmasked the puppet master, the master manipulator who has woven their web of control over the world for centuries. We have seen the devastating consequences of their manipulation and the power they wield to divide, destroy, and deceive. But we have also witnessed the strength and resilience of those who dare to challenge their influence, who refuse to be mere puppets in their grand design.

Our journey has taken us through the depths of self-reflection, where we have questioned our beliefs, biases, and assumptions. We have confronted the limitations of a fixed mindset, the destructive power of fear-driven mentalities, and the hollow pursuit of materialism and consumerism. Through self-reflection, we have begun to break free from the chains that bind us, opening ourselves up to new possibilities and a more authentic way of living.

Building and nurturing relationships has been another crucial aspect of our journey. We have discovered the transformative power of genuine connections and the importance of empathy, compassion, and understanding in bridging divides and fostering unity. Through the stories of individuals, we have seen how embracing diversity and acknowledging the value of every individual can create a ripple effect of positive change.

The foundation of God's word has guided us throughout this exploration, serving as a beacon of light in the darkness. It has given us wisdom, guidance, and a moral compass to navigate the world's complexities. We have come to understand that true liberation comes not from pursuing power and money but from aligning ourselves with the divine purpose and embracing love, justice, and kindness.

We have followed the LIGHT Pathway, a transformative framework for personal growth and societal change. We have explored the pillars of Luminary Foundation, Inclusive Bonds, Generous Empathy, Harmonious Evolution, and Transformative Growth. These pillars have guided us in breaking free from the shackles of harmful worldviews, cultivating a sense of unity, and igniting the transformation within ourselves and our communities.

Standing at the precipice of change, we have confronted the puppet master and their insidious influence. We have exposed their secrets, manipulation tactics, and the harm they inflict on humanity. But in doing so, we have also discovered our power to resist, to break free from their control, and to reclaim our autonomy. Through unity and collective action, we can dismantle the puppet master's web and build a world founded on truth, justice, and compassion.

At this moment, we find ourselves on the cusp of transformation. The unseen chains that have bound us far too long are beginning to fracture. We have embraced the call to action, rising above the limitations of the past and envisioning a future defined by unity and generational healing. It is a future where our diversity is celebrated, love and empathy guide our actions, and a collective desire for the well-being and happiness of all overshadows the pursuit of power and money.